AWAKEN, CHILDREN!

Dialogues With
Sri Sri Mata Amritanandamayi

VOLUME VIII

SWAMI AMRITASWARUPANANDA

MATA AMRITANANDAMAYI CENTER
San Ramon, California

AWAKEN, CHILDREN!
Volume VIII

PUBLISHED BY:
Mata Amritanandamayi Center
P.O. Box 613
San Ramon, CA 94583-0613
Tel: (510) 537-9417

FIRST PRINTING May 1996

ALSO AVAILABLE FROM:
Mata Amritanandamayi Mission Trust
Amritapuri P.O., Kollam Dt., Kerala
INDIA 690525

ISBN 1-879410-66-4

This Book Is Humbly Offered At The
LOTUS FEET OF HER HOLINESS
SRI SRI MATA AMRITANANDAMAYI
The Resplendent Luminary Immanent
In the Hearts Of All Beings

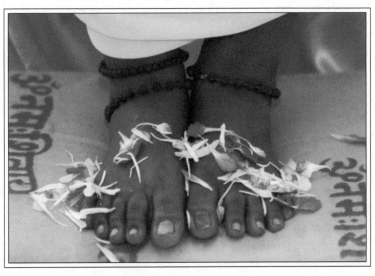

Vandeham-saccidānandam-bhāvātītam-jagatgurum |
Nityam-pūrnam-nirākāram-nirgunam-svātmasamsthitam | |

I prostrate to the Universal Teacher, Who is Satchidananda (Pure
Being-Knowledge-Absolute Bliss), Who is beyond all differences,
Who is eternal, all-full, attributeless, formless and ever-centered in
the Self.

Saptasāgaraparyantam-tīrthasnānaphalam-tu-yat |
Gurupādapayōvindōh-sahasrāmśena-tatphalam | |

Whatever merit is acquired by one, through pilgrimages and from
bathing in the Sacred Waters extending to the seven seas, cannot be equal to even one thousandth part of the merit derived
from partaking the water with which the Guru's Feet are washed.

GURU GITA
Verses 157, 87

CONTENTS

SONGS

INTRODUCTION

Through this book, the eighth volume of *Awaken Children*, Mother's infinite wisdom is flowing once again. When a perfect Master like Mother speaks, it is Pure Consciousness speaking; it is Krishna, Rama, Buddha and Christ speaking; it is all the supreme masters of the past, present and future speaking. It is the Voice of God Himself. In fact, Mother's words are not only words, for they contain a consciousness of their own. Mother's unconditional spiritual energy can be experienced in each word that She utters, if one reads with a meditative and contemplative mind.

By speaking to us through this book, our beloved Mother is inspiring and uplifting us, in giving us a taste of the Truth, which will eventually help us merge into the indescribable Ocean of *sat-chit-ananda* (being-consciousness-bliss). Above all, the absolutely charming and purifying presence of this great Master, is the most fertile soil out of which the flowers of our hearts may open up and blossom.

Mother never talks about Her greatness. But this mysterious phenomenon that is Mother is an irresistible Power. The divine love and compassion Mother spreads is inimitable. She literally radiates peace and joy. Her existence is complete and perfect. Mother's words are shining rays of the

Truth which carry the immortal message of the Absolute
Reality to us.

We can continue to study any amount of scriptures, but
nothing will happen, no spiritual progress will be achieved,
unless we find a spiritual Master such as Mother. If we can
simply be in Mother's presence, we will experience the divine fragrance of sat-chit-ananda flowing out of Her in a
never-ending stream; the presence of God will become tan-
gible to us, and without being taught, we will learn how to
be our true Self.

Swami Amritaswarupananda

M.A. Math, Amritapuri

Most of the events in this book took place during the year 1986. A few of the events, however, occurred in 1984 and 1985.

CHAPTER ONE

THE PLAYFUL MOTHER

Mother looked like a beautiful dark-blue statue. She was sitting in a deeply absorbed state of samadhi in front of the new Ashram building which was under construction. Mother was surrounded by most of the Ashram residents and a visiting family who were all looking intently at Her. The sun shone bright and warm; it seemed to be gazing down to get a glimpse of Mother and to caress Her body with its beautiful golden rays. As everyone sat contemplating Mother's enchanting countenance, She opened Her eyes and smiled at them. When Mother smiles, the heart of everyone opens up, and one cannot help but smile as well. Her sweet smile has a wonderful healing effect. Without saying a word, Mother can express Her Divinity through Her look, smile or touch. Sitting in Her presence is like experiencing direct communion with God. This holy place, Amritapuri, which is constantly illumined by Mother's presence, where one can experience a never ending stream of supreme love and the depth of true knowledge, reminds one of the *gurukulas*[1] of the ancient *rishis*.

Mother began to play with a little girl who was barely two

---

[1] Hermitages where children of ancient times used to be sent for twelve years to study with a master.

years old, and who belonged to the visiting family. The little
girl had a piece of a sweet in her hands. Mother stretched out
Her right palm and said to her, "Give some to Amma." The
child gazed at Mother for a long time with a wondrous look
in her eyes. All of a sudden she turned around and ran towards her parents with a giggle. Mother followed her, picked
her up and forcibly carried her back to the place where She
had been sitting. The child sat calmly on Mother's lap. Now
Mother opened Her mouth and wanted the child to feed Her
with some of the sweet. This time the child smiled beautifully at Mother and brought the sweet very close to Mother's
mouth. Mother was about to take a bite when the child
suddenly withdrew the sweet, scrambled down from Mother's
lap and again ran away. This evoked much laughter. Mother
was very amused by this and She burst into peals of laughter. One of the devotees remarked, "She is like you, Amma."
The devotee was referring to Krishna Bhava, when Mother
used to feed *prasad* to the devotees in a playful mood which
reminded one of Krishna's childhood sportings.

The Holy Mother was not willing to give up that easily.
She adamantly followed the child, caught hold of her and
brought her back to the same spot. It looked as if Mother
Herself had become an innocent child. The little girl who
was again sitting on Mother's lap was also enjoying the play.

Mother again opened Her mouth wanting the child to feed Her. The parents encouraged the child saying, "Kunji (little one), give some to Amma! You love Amma so much, don't you?"

Gazing at Mother's beautiful face, the child once again brought the sweet close to Mother's mouth. She was about to withdraw her hand and run away again, but this time Mother took hold of her little hand and took a tiny bite from the sweet. This was too much for the little girl. She began to cry, expressing her anger and protest by throwing the sweet onto Mother's lap. Seeing the child's innocent behavior, Mother again burst into laughter, followed by much laughter from all those present. Even the child's parents joined in. This made the little girl cry even louder. She protested more strongly by throwing herself down and rolling on the ground. Mother looked at her and said, "She feels that she is being teased." But soon Mother picked her up from the ground and consoled her. She asked Bri. Gayatri[2] to bring another sweet for her. The child was happy to receive a fresh piece of sweet from Mother, but she also wanted the old one. She now had two pieces in her hands. The child stopped crying as she sat on Mother's lap. Somebody commented, "The little girl doesn't want to discard the old piece because

---

[2] Swamini Amrita Prana

it's Amma's prasad." When the atmosphere calmed down, the child again looked up at Mother's face. All of a sudden she brought both the pieces of sweet up to Mother's mouth and wholeheartedly offered them to Mother. She kept her little hands in the same position until Mother opened Her mouth and took a small bite from each of the sweets. The child again wanted to feed Mother. But Mother said lovingly, "No, no, my darling! This is for you! Amma has had enough." Mother affectionately hugged and kissed the little one, and holding the child on Her lap, Mother began to sing *Chilanka Ketti*, as if She were singing a lullaby. . .

> O my lotus-eyed One
> Tie on Your anklets and come running!
> Come dancing!
> We are singing Your divine Name
> As we go in search of Your tender feet.
>
> O Devaki's Son
> Radha's own Life
> O Kesava, Hare, Madhava[3]
> O Slayer of Pootana
> Destroyer of sins
> Child of Gokula, come running!
> O Cowherd Boy, come dancing!

---

[3] Names of Krishna.

O Slayer of Kamsa
Who danced on the serpent Kaliya
O Kesava, Hare, Madhava
Affectionate to those
Who take refuge in You
O Embodiment of Aum
Protector of those in danger
Come running!
O Melody of Bliss
Come dancing!

O Protector of the Pandavas
Destroyer of sins
O Kesava, Hare, Madhava
Protector of Arjuna
Destroyer of ignorance
O Kesava, Hare, Madhava
O Nectar of the Gita
Come running!
O Bliss of the heart
Come dancing!

The little girl sat quietly on Mother's lap for a while, and then Mother let her go to her parents. Mother lay down on the ground with Her head resting on Gayatri's lap. One of the brahmacharis asked Mother a question.

"Almost all children cry when they are born. But Amma, You smiled when You came into this world. Is there any significance to this?"

Mother: "A newborn baby usually cries because, to the baby, this world is a strange place. Having spent nine long months in the mother's womb, the child suddenly finds itself in a new world. While in the womb, the baby has been in great discomfort caused by the intestinal filth, the heat of the mother's digestive system and the constant movements of the processes of her body. The child suffers like this for nine months and nine days before it comes out into the world in a painful crush and suffocating discomfort. And now, the newborn child again feels discomfort, caused by the unfamiliar atmospheric pressure and the strange surroundings. For the baby, this is a strange, unknown world. It therefore cries out of sheer despair.

"But Amma had no feelings of strangeness when She came into this world. Everything was so utterly familiar to Her; and when one knows everything about the world, one can only smile. When one beholds the entire universe as a play of consciousness, what else can one do but smile? When you have the power, the penetrating eyes, with which to see the Reality behind all outer appearances, you can only smile. You then perceive only the changeless within the ever-changing exterior. You don't see the outer shell of the seed—you see the whole potential tree within the seed. In short, you behold Reality, the true nature of everything. Once you are able to see the Truth, nothing is unknown or strange to you; you are familiar with the entire universe, and you smile, not occasionally, but continuously. Your life becomes a big smile. You constantly smile at everything—not only during happy moments, but also during unhappy moments. You even smile at death. This is spirituality. Spirituality is a deep and genuine smile at all the situations in life.

"When do people feel sad and desperate? When they find themselves in strange situations, and they don't know what to do or where to go, when they feel helpless and there is nobody to turn to, and in the face of failure, loss, disease, and death. At such times, they are pushed into a strange, helpless state. They are overcome by despair and they cry because they don't know anything; they don't know any methods by which to overcome their situations.

"But as far as a perfect soul is concerned, he knows the secret mystery of life. He knows that everything that happens around him is just a play of consciousness. His eyes can penetrate beyond the three periods of time and behold Reality. He knows the Truth out of which the whole world has emerged. He knows the true existence, the Ground, of the world; he knows where everything is moving and where it finally merges. This knowledge allows him to smile heartily at everything. The Perfect Soul can smile at everything because of his omniscience.

SMILING EYES

"When you are all-knowing, when your eyes can penetrate beyond the past, the present and the future, then your eyes will also smile, and not just your lips. Look at the picture of Kali dancing on Shiva's chest. Even though She looks fierce, there is a smile in Her eyes. That smile is the smile of omniscience. Krishna had smiling eyes. All great masters have uniquely smiling eyes. When your eyes have the power to penetrate beyond the surface of existence, then your eyes will radiate with joy. You see the truth—that which lies within—and therefore you smile. The outer surface is a lie. But now the false surface cannot deceive you any longer, because you have learned the art of penetrating and seeing right through everything. Your mere look exposes the outer thief and liar. It then disappears and the Truth comes to light. The meaning of the smile is, 'I know the Truth.' It is a sign of perfect omniscience."

At the end of the conversation Mother suddenly rolled over onto the bare ground. The residents who were sitting there were familiar with Mother's strange moods and they quickly moved out of the way. They knew that during such occasions, Mother didn't want anyone to touch Her and She preferred to lie on the bare ground. Mother was lying with

Her eyes focused towards the sky. She raised Her right hand and held it in a divine mudra, and She was repeatedly making strange sounds as if She were conversing with someone in an unknown language. Mother was lying absolutely still. After a few minutes She closed Her eyes and Her face lit up with a wonderful smile, which made Her entire face shine with an extraordinary brilliance. Mother lay in this position for about ten minutes. She then uttered Her usual mantra, "Shiva, Shiva." She got up and walked towards the old temple. Having entered the temple She closed the doors behind Her and remained there for half an hour.

A PINCH AND A CARESS

The description Mother had just given about Herself and Her omniscience gives us a glimpse of the tremendous awareness Mother had of Her godly nature even at birth. Hearing that great truth from Her own lips is a thrilling experience.

Mother's statement that a Mahatma is able to penetrate the three periods of time, is reminiscent of an incident that happened to a devotee who came to meet Mother for the first time. The man, who lived in Bangalore, had come to see Mother together with his wife. The long line of devotees moved slowly towards Mother, who, as usual, was receiving

Her children one by one. When his turn came, Mother gave him a hard pinch without uttering a word. He got very angry at this, to the point where he was boiling with rage. There was a reason for his anger. When he was a young boy, he had a strong aversion to being pinched and he protested vehemently whenever he was pinched by his parents or teachers. He even quarreled with his teachers who sometimes pinched him as a minor punishment for not studying his lessons. He would tell them, "You can beat me with a stick if you want or send me out of the classroom, but don't ever pinch me!" So on this day, when he came up to Mother and She pinched him, it made him extremely angry. But before he had a chance to protest, Mother pulled his head onto Her lap; and as he lay on Her lap, Mother caressed his hair and combed it softly with Her fingers. This experience touched him so deeply that all his anger vanished, and he was in blissful tears. There was a specific reason for this feeling as well. He was in the habit of sometimes asking small children to stroke his hair exactly the way Mother was now doing with Her fingers. He loved it so much that when he was lying in bed, he used to ask the children to gently comb his hair with their fingers, so that he would sleep well. Because he knew that he liked it more than anything, it didn't take much time for him to realize that Mother is omniscient.

When Mother first pinched him, and then, a moment later, combed his hair with Her fingers, he had a sudden revelation that, "Here is somebody who knows everything about me, my likes and my dislikes, and to whom my life is an open book." This experience was all that was needed for him to surrender everything at Her feet.

The devotee said, "When Mother lifted my head up from Her lap, I looked at Her face in utter wonderment. She was smiling at me and She said, 'Being pinched is what you hate the most, and having your hair stroked is what you like the most, isn't it?' By pinching me and stroking my hair like that, I strongly felt that Mother was saying, 'Son, Amma knows everything about you.' I was tongue-tied and completely taken aback. Thereafter, I never doubted Mother's omniscience."

CHAPTER TWO

RELATIONSHIPS

*T*oday, before the evening bhajans, Mother came down and sat at the western side of the temple. She was soon surrounded by the residents and a few house-holder devotees. One of the householders, a bank manager, asked Mother a question about relationships.

Mother: "A true relationship can be developed only if there is proper understanding between a husband and wife, between friends, or whoever is involved in a relationship of any kind. There are different passages in life. Marriage is one such passage, and it is one of the most important ones there is. For a person who lives in the world (i.e. a householder), to be able to live a full, productive life, he or she must pass through the passage of marriage with as much love, intimacy, caring and commitment as possible. Married life, if it is lived with the proper love and understanding, will help awaken the feminine within a man, and the masculine within a woman. This balance can eventually help both of them reach the final goal of eternal freedom.

"If the couple takes the necessary steps, making the effort

to understand and respect each other's feelings, they will be able to live their lives fully. They should be willing to forgive and forget each other's faults and weaknesses. Married life can be a rich field of learning that teaches the couple to develop such qualities as patience and humility.

"In Indian society this is easier, as Indian women tend to be more yielding in nature and less aggressive. The ego of a man is kept in check by the humility and patience of a woman. Although modern society is changing at a rapid pace, the basic culture of Indian society remains the same. But if there is to be a proper balance and sense of harmony in married life, men should try not to be aggressive, arrogant, or self-important in front of women, and they shouldn't try to dominate them. In India men often think they have the right to control women, and that a woman should never be ahead of a man in any way. This is clearly the wrong attitude, which is due to the lack of proper understanding of the culture which was founded by the ancient saints and seers.

MOTHERHOOD
GOD'S WONDERFUL GIFT TO WOMEN

"A woman should be respected and her feelings should to be given proper consideration. Her maternal qualities should

be recognized and she should be given a higher, well de-
served position in society, along with men. At the same time,
she should know that the greatest gift God has bestowed on
her is the gift of motherhood, the right to give birth and to
raise a child with the proper care, love and affection. It is a
unique gift, and it is hers alone. To give birth to the greatest
people born on this earth, the divine incarnations, the great
leaders, philosophers, and scientists—to give birth to all the
eminent souls and to all of mankind—this is one of the
greatest blessings of all. Why has God given women this
wonderful gift? Because they alone have the capacity to express such qualities as love, compassion, caring, and patience,
in all its fullness and beauty. Every woman should know
this and try to comprehend the significance of this blessing.
But it would seem that women are slowly forgetting this truth;
and if they ignore this fundamental and indispensable quality within themselves, our society will be turned upside down.
It is therefore vitally important that women recognize these
qualities within themselves.

"It is mostly in western society that women are forgetting their feminine qualities. In the name of equality, many
women are disregarding this most priceless blessing they have
been given. In the West, as opposed to Indian society, women
are more aggressive and less yielding. As western women try

to catch up with men in all areas of life, they do not realize that they are sacrificing an essential part of their nature. The result of this is total chaos and confusion, both in the outer and inner life. Amma is not saying that a woman shouldn't do the same things that men do—she can and she should, and women have an immense inner power—but it should never be done at the cost of sacrificing her essential being. Going against nature is destructive; it is dangerous for the person in question as well as for society as a whole.

"In the West both men and women tend to be aggressive. Aggression, however, is negative energy. Sometimes it may be needed in life, but not in relationships, not in married life. When two poles are negative, only negative energy is produced, resulting in complete disharmony and disruption.

"In western society both husband and wife try to control each other; they believe it is their right to do so. In the constant clash and tug-of-war that follows, the love and the beauty of the relationship is destroyed.

"Love is not aggressive, and neither is life. They cannot be forced. Life is love. Without the feeling of love, through which we experience true life, our existence becomes dry and empty, like a robot. Life and love are interdependent—if there is no love, you are ignoring life itself."

MARRIED LIFE

Question: "Amma, why is there no real love in married life? What causes the conflicts and the friction?"

Mother: "There is a serious lack of understanding between the husband and wife. In most cases the couple won't even make an attempt to understand each other. For the development of a true relationship to take place, a basic understanding of human nature, the nature of men and women, is essential. A man should know what a woman is really like, and vice versa. But, instead, they dwell in two isolated worlds with no connection between them. They are like two separate islands with no link between them, not even a ferry service.

"Men are mostly intellectually centered, while women tend to be more emotional. They dwell in two different centers, along two parallel lines. No real meeting takes place within them. How, then, can there be any love between the two? If the one says yes, the other will undoubtedly say no. You will never hear the harmonious blending of yes and yes or no and no in unison. Their different natures should be understood and accepted, and each one, both husband and wife, should make a conscious effort to reach out to the other's feelings, to the heart, and then try to work out their problems with this understanding as their foundation. They shouldn't try to control each other. They shouldn't say to each other, 'I say yes, and therefore you should also say yes.'

"Any such attitude should be dropped, for it will only lead to anger and even hatred. The love in such a relationship will be very superficial. If the gulf between these two centers, the intellect and emotions (mind), can be bridged, the sweet music of love will spring forth from the depths within them. This unifying factor is spirituality. If you look at our ancestors, you will see that their marriages were generally more loving than such relationships are today. There was much more love and harmony in their lives, because they had a better understanding of the spiritual principles and their implications in day-to-day life.

"Amma has heard the following story. A married woman decided that she wanted a pet. But her husband was against it. One day when he was away, she went to a pet shop and bought a monkey. Needless to say, her husband was angry when he came home and found the monkey in the house. He asked her, 'What is that creature going to eat?'

'What else but the same food that we eat,' she replied.

'And where is it going to sleep?'

'Where else but in the same bed where we sleep,' came the reply.

'But are you not worried about the smell!'

'No! Don't worry, if I could bear it for the last twenty years, I'm sure this poor animal can bear it as well!'"

Everyone burst into laughter as Mother finished the story. Mother continued, "It is very rare to find a truly loving relationship. The love between a married couple is usually only skin deep. If one of them says 'yes,' the other will make it a point to say 'no.' Children, learn to respect each other's feelings. Learn to listen to each other's problems with love and concern. When you listen to your partner, he or she should be able to feel that you are genuinely interested and that you would sincerely like to help. Your partner should feel your care and concern, your respect and admiration. An open acceptance of the other is needed, and there should be no reservations. Still, conflicts are bound to occur; misunderstandings and disagreements may arise; but later, one should be able to say, 'I'm sorry, please forgive me. I didn't mean it." Or you could say, "I love you and I'm deeply concerned about you—don't ever think otherwise. I'm sorry, I shouldn't have said what I said; in my anger I lost my temper and my power of discrimination." Such soothing words will help to heal any hurt feelings; it will also contribute to a deep feeling of love between you, even after a big quarrel."

Mother stopped and said, "Balumon (Balu, my son), sing a song." Br. Srikumar was asked to bring the harmonium.

They started chanting, *Mauna Ghanamrita*. Mother leaned Her head against Bri. Gayatri's shoulder and listened to the bhajan with Her eyes half closed. The blissful, radiant smile on Mother's face made it clear that She was in an indrawn state.

> *In the abode of impenetrable Silence*
> *Of eternal Beauty and Peace*
> *Where the mind of Gautama Buddha*
> *was dissolved,*
> *In the Effulgence that destroys all bonds,*
> *On the Shore of Bliss*
> *Which lies beyond the reach of thought. . .*
>
> *In the Knowledge that bestows eternal*
> *harmony,*
> *The Abode without beginning or end,*
> *The Bliss known only when*
> *The movements of the mind subside,*
> *At the Seat of Power,*
> *The Region of Perfect Consciousness. . .*
>
> *At the Goal which bestows the sweet state*
> *Of eternal non-duality*
> *Described as' Thou art That,'*
> *That is the place where I long to reach;*
> *But I can only do so*
> *Through Your Grace.*

After the singing had stopped, Mother continued to lean against Gayatri's shoulder. When She eventually stirred and sat up, one of the devotees said to Her, "Amma, you were talking about relationships."

Mother then continued to speak.

RECOGNIZE AND ADMIRE
THE GOOD QUALITIES IN EACH OTHER

"Children, as ordinary human beings, everyone has both good and bad qualities. Always try to recognize and admire the good qualities in each other. Whenever you are talking to others about your partner, try to highlight his or her good qualities; don't ever mention the weaknesses in front of others. Whatever your weaknesses may be, they should remain a secret between the two of you. You should work out your problems together with a positive attitude, without provoking or hurting each other with accusations. First of all, we should become aware of our own weaknesses, because this is the best way to remove them. Never use your partner's faults as a weapon against him or her. When you are pointing out a weakness, do so lovingly and with every intention of eradicating it in a positive way from your lives. These weaknesses are blocks which prevent you from expressing yourselves fully. See these blocks as obstructions and learn to remove them.

"Recently, a devotee, who is a hospital administrator working in Bombay, was talking about a problem they had in the hospital, concerning cleanliness. Most people in the North are in the habit of chewing pan, a concoction made of betel leaves, aracanut and other ingredients. It is their practice to chew the pan and then, without a second thought, spit out the bright red substance wherever they happen to be standing. The four corners of the hospital elevators were splattered all over with the crimson spittle of visitors. The hospital administration had a meeting, in which they tried to come up with a solution to this problem. Finally, they decided to install mirrors in all four corners of the elevators. As soon as this step had been taken, people stopped spitting in the elevators. What made them stop? Undoubtedly it was the sight of their own image as they were spitting, being reflected in the mirrors. Once they saw how ugly it was, they couldn't bring themselves to do it again, and so they stopped.

"Similarly, try to look at your own faults and you will automatically eradicate them. By seeing your own weaknesses and bad habits you become aware of how ugly they are. Your weaknesses lie hidden in the dark, but as you look at them they are brought out into the light.

"Our great ancestors have given us wonderful examples on how to recognize and respect others for their good qualities.

"One of the *Ramayanas* describes a beautiful incident in which Lord Rama set an unforgettable example of humility, by recognizing the great sacrifice of Urmila, Lakshmana's chaste wife. When Lakshmana, Rama's brother, followed him to the forest during the period of Rama's exile, Urmila was forced to spend fourteen years in Ayodhya, experiencing the terrible pain of separation from her husband, whom she adored. Rama had brought His holy consort, Sita, along with Him. But Lakshmana had to leave his wife behind in Ayodhya. Urmila lived a life of great self-sacrifice, spending her days and nights constantly thinking about her husband. One day, when Rama finally returned to Ayodhya, he was seen walking towards Urmila's private chamber. Out of curiosity, Lakshmana followed him and secretly watched what the Lord was doing. What Lakshmana witnessed literally made him burst into tears. Urmila was lying fast asleep on her bed. The Lord joined his palms together in a gesture of reverence and walked round the bed thrice, after which he prostrated on the floor in front of her feet, just as people do in temples.

"Later when Lakshmana asked Sri Rama to explain the meaning of this act, the Lord replied, 'Urmila is worthy of the greatest respect and appreciation. The great sacrifice she has made deserves our admiration. I simply wanted to acknowledge her but without her knowing it, because if she had been awake, she wouldn't have let me do it. That is why I went to her when she was asleep.'

"Such great examples shown to us by the mahatmas should be remembered and followed. This will bring harmony, love and peace both to our inner and outer lives. It will remove any discordant notes that may exist in a relationship and in married life. Men should never be arrogant or reluctant to recognize a woman's good qualities. Their attitude is very wrong indeed, if they think, 'After all, she is only a woman.'

"Look at how meaningless modern relationships are. There is rarely any true love between a married couple. There is too much judgment, fear, and suspicion to make a loving relationship possible. Due to lack of love and proper understanding, relationships have become no more than skin deep.

"Amma recently heard a funny story which comes to mind. Two young men met on the street. One of them said to the other, 'You lucky man! You have won yourself a pretty girlfriend. Tell me, what does she think about you?'

'She thinks I have a great personality, that I am a gifted singer and a talented painter,' came the reply.

'And what about you? What attracts you to her?'

'That she thinks I have a great personality, that I am a gifted singer and a talented painter.'"

When the laughter had quieted down, Mother asked for

a song. One of the householder devotees sang the song,
Amritamayi Anandamayi. . .

> *O Goddess of Nectar*
> *Goddess of Immortal Bliss*
> *O Mother Amritanandamayi*
> *O Goddess of Nectar*
> *Goddess of Eternal Bliss. . .*
>
> *O Mother*
> *As You watch Your children shed tears*
> *Your heart melts with concern.*
>
> *O compassionate Mother*
> *Lovingly You caress Your children*
> *And You feed them*
> *The milk of tenderness.*
>
> *O Mother, with the hue of an emerald gem*
> *Come and dwell in my heart!*
> *Your Lotus Feet are the sole refuge*
> *of this poor one.*
>
> *You shine forth from within*
> *As the inner eye of the external eye;*
> *You are the Mother of Kanna*
> *You are the Mother of the whole Universe*
> *The Goddess of the Universe.*

THE SIGN OF A TRUE RELATIONSHIP

After the song, Mother continued to enlighten Her children on the same subject.

Question: "What are the signs of a true relationship?"

Mother: "When two people identify with each other, it is the sign of a true relationship. The intensity of love depends on the amount of identification there is between people. Suppose someone were to ask you, 'Which one of your friends do you love the most, a or b or c?' Perhaps you'd have to think about it for a while, or perhaps you wouldn't have to think at all; you would spontaneously say, 'I like a the most. He is my best friend.' What does it mean when you say that you like a the most? It means that you are more identified with a than with b or c, doesn't it? A true relationship, or true love, is based on the amount of identification one has with someone. However, it isn't something that can be measured, for it is a deep feeling, something that happens within. As the identification intensifies, that sense of oneness becomes manifest externally as well. Your heart overflows with love and expresses itself through your words and actions. At its peak, even your bodies will bear a close resemblance. This rarely happens in worldly relationships. In a spiritual relationship, however, it happens in a clear, profound way. It happens, for example, to a disciple who has completely surrendered to his spiritual master, and whose heart is filled with love and devotion towards his master.

"This is exactly what happened to the gopis of Vrindavan. By constantly thinking of Sri Krishna, the gopis became like Him. At one stage the gopis used to say to each other, 'Friend, look at me. I am Krishna. I walk like Him, don't I? Can't you see the divine flute in my hands and the peacock feather in my crown?'

"Amma knows a married couple who have developed this sense of identification with each other. They look like twins—even their voices and movements are similar. Amma has known them for a long time. They are the ideal couple; the mutual love, respect, understanding, patience, and forgiveness they have towards each other is extraordinary. So it can happen even in a worldly relationship, even in married life, provided you have the right attitude.

"In such deep love, even your thought patterns will be the same. For example, a husband may think of something without saying a word about it. Yet somehow his wife is aware of it. He thinks of something and his wife says the same thing, or he wishes to do something and his wife suddenly expresses the same wish. It is Sunday. He is sitting in his work room trying to get some urgent work done. He happens to feel very tired, but he can't go and take a nap because the work has to be finished and lying on his boss's desk by the very next day. As he struggles to keep his eyes open, he thinks to himself, 'I need a cup of strong coffee.' But he doesn't want to go and ask his wife to make it because he knows that she is busy preparing the Sunday lunch. It is not his habit to drink coffee at that time of day; and yet, to his surprise, a moment later his wife enters the room and hands him a cup of coffee. He asks, 'How on earth did you know that I needed a cup of coffee?' She smiles and replies, 'I just felt that you'd like a cup, that's all.' This sort of thing happens during certain moments in a relationship, and it can be developed, provided the couple have the right feeling and understanding between each other. It will then grow and eventually manifest through all their thoughts and actions.

"If this can happen in a normal relationship, the identification or sense of oneness that happens in the Guru-sishya relationship is incomparably greater.

"Gayatri had an experience which is worth mentioning. Once, Amma was working outside with the ashramites. When Amma later returned to Her room, Her hands were dirty. Amma wanted to wash Her hands, so She asked Gayatri to bring Her some soap and water. But instead of bringing Her the soap and water, Gayatri started washing her own hands under the bathroom tap. Lakshmi saw her standing in the bathroom washing her own hands while Amma was waiting for the soap and water. Lakshmi had to remind her that Amma was waiting for Her hands to be washed. When Gayatri heard Lakshmi's words, she came back to her senses. Realizing that she was washing her own hands instead of Amma's, she exclaimed, 'O my God, I thought I was washing Mother's hands!' She felt perplexed and glanced at Amma with a guilty expression. But Amma understood what had happened. This happened to Gayatri at a particular moment when she was able to forget herself. But the power to experience that oneness, that total identification, is always there within us.

"A true relationship is possible only when one is able to let go of all one's preconceived ideas and prejudices, and when one stops being possessed by the past. Your mind is the past. Stop clinging to the past and you will be free and peaceful. To cling to the past is like living in the dark. We all want to be in the light. Stop fighting the past, stop reacting to it, and you will be in the light. You will then clearly be able to see everything that is happening within you. With such a clear vision it is possible to form a true relationship."

As Mother spoke, the sun was slowly descending on the western horizon for its usual dip in the deep blue ocean. Just as the sun works tirelessly and selflessly to sustain life on

earth, Mother, the Spiritual Sun, is constantly working hard
to inspire Her children through Her profound words, Her
divine presence, Her compassionate embrace, and Her el-
evating bhajans. She touches the heart of everyone by expressing Her incomparable love and compassion with Her
whole being, helping everyone to open up fully and to, in
their turn, spread a sweet, divine fragrance and beauty all
around.

When Mother had finished talking, She got up from
Her seat and stood with Her arms outstretched towards the
sky. She called out, "Shivane!" For some time She remained
standing in that position with Her eyes closed, and then She
walked over to the temple. It was time for bhajans. Mother
was about to carry Her children on the wings of Her ecstatic,
melodious song. Blissfully Mother began to sing the song, *Anjana
Sridhara. . .*

> *O Sridhara,*
> *Collyrium-hued and beautiful*
> *I salute You with joined palms.*
> *Victory to Krishna,*
> *Salutations to Him!*
>
> *O Krishna,*
> *Who was born on earth*

As a Divine Child,
Protect me in every way.

O darling Krishna,
Please destroy the grief in my heart.
O Cowherd Boy,
Lotus-eyed Krishna,
Come and shine in my heart!

O Krishna!
I am filled with the desire
To see the beauty
Of Your dear, auspicious form.

O Cowherd Boy,
Please come running,
And play Your flute!

CHAPTER THREE

THE SECRET OF A CHILD'S BEAUTY

ℬecause the new temple was being constructed, the Ashram premises looked rather messy. Mother, however, insisted that all the bricks, sand, and other construction materials be kept in an organized way. Whenever She came down from Her room, Mother Herself took the initiative and started cleaning the grounds. As far as Mother was concerned, no work was too menial for Her. She could be seen carrying the bricks and sand on Her head. A moment later, Mother would grab a shovel and begin to fill the baskets with sand. This morning when Mother came down, She asked the residents to bring baskets and tools, and She began to clean the grounds. Within a few minutes the entire Ashram population were on their feet ready to work. As Mother worked along with the residents, She sang the song, *Entu Chevo Yedu Chevo. . .*

> *Alas! What am I to do?*
> *The Son of Nanda is not to be found anywhere.*

Did He get up early this morning
And go to the forest to graze the cows?
Or—O God!—did He break His legs
Fighting with the other children?

Or, perhaps, he has been running here
and there
And fallen into a ditch. . . .

Everyone responded and sang the chorus of the song. Mother was setting a perfect example of doing work as a form of worship. The work continued for more than an hour. As Mother's presence adds beauty and charm to any given situation, there was now an atmosphere of great joy amongst the participants. When the cleaning was over, Mother sat down, surrounded by the Ashram residents and householder devotees. While everyone was relaxing, one of the residents raised a question. "Spiritual masters all over the world use the small child as an example of the ultimate state of Perfection. What is so special about a child in connection with spirituality?"

Mother: "Look at a child. The child is not at all concerned about the past or the future. Whatever the child does, is done with total participation. The child is fully present in whatever he does, he cannot do anything partially. Children live in the present; this is why people feel so drawn to them. You cannot really dislike a child, because the ugliness of the ego is not present in the child.

"A child can attract anyone's attention; even the most cold-hearted person will have some feelings towards a child, unless the person is a demonic monster. This attraction is due to the innocence of the child. When you are free from the grip of the ego, you, yourself, will become as innocent and playful as a child.

"Most human beings live with one foot planted in the dead past, and the other in the future, which is not real. The future is an unreal dream which has yet to happen. You cannot be sure that it will actually happen in your case. The future is uncertain; it may or may not occur, and yet, the most intelligent human beings constantly worry and dream about the future, or they brood and cry recollecting the dead fossils of the past. Both the past and the future should disappear. Only then will you be able to live in this moment; for, it is in this moment that you experience reality. This moment alone is real. The past and the future are unreal.

"Just as a child lives fully in the present, when you love, let your whole being be present in that love, without any divisions or reservations. Don't do anything partially, do it fully by being in the present moment. Don't brood on the past, and don't cling to it. Forget the past and stop dreaming about the future. Express yourself by being fully present, right now. Nothing, neither the regrets of the past nor the anxieties about the future, should interfere with the flow as you express your inner feelings. Let go of everything, and let your whole being flow through your mood. This is exactly what a child does.

"A child doesn't have any attachments to the past, nor does he worry about the future. When a child says, 'Mummy, I like you so much!' he really means it. Through his kisses, looks, and loving ways he expresses himself with his whole being. The child doesn't recall the scolding or thrashing he was given yesterday, nor is he upset because the toy he so badly wanted wasn't bought for him; and he has no worries about tomorrow. He doesn't hold onto anything. The child simply loves and forgets. A child can never do anything partially. Whenever he does anything, he is fully present. Doing something partially is possible only when there is an ego.

"Whatever a child does is not related to any memories. The child is in the present moment, and whether he is feeling love or anger, it is being fully expressed. But he will soon forget it and pass on to the next moment. A child's expressions, whether it be anger or love, are never caused by attachment. That is why even the anger of a child has a certain beauty. It is purely natural and spontaneous, and whatever is expressed spontaneously, without any interference of the ego, has a beauty and charm of its own. But you have to be innocent to be that spontaneous. This is why even the anger of a Mahatma is beautiful, because the Mahatma is absolutely pure and innocent. His expressions are spontaneous, direct, and utterly natural. He is not reacting out of the past. He just is, right here, in this moment.

"A grownup's anger is ugly. Nobody likes a person when he is angry. But the anger of a child is different. When a child is angry, the father, mother or someone else will lift the child into their arms and embrace him. They will kiss the child and do all they can to calm him down. Whereas the anger of a grownup is repulsive and will arouse the anger in others, a child's anger invokes our love and sympathy. It is the presence of the ego in the grownup, and its absence in the child, that makes the difference.

"You can only be attached if you have an ego. The ego makes you attached to the past, and as long as the ego's attachment to the past exists, you cannot express anything fully. Your every word and action will be tainted by the ego. The past creeps up before you and creates a fence between yourself and whatever you do or say. Whatever you wish to express is first filtered through the fence of the past; thus the child, or the innocence within, is completely blocked.

"A child has no ego, no past or future. The child has no attachments, and because of this, he is able to express himself fully, without any prejudices or preconceived ideas.

REAL GROWTH AND MATURITY

"Grownups believe they have grown up, that they should no longer be like children, and that childlike qualities are something to be ashamed of. But what really has grown up in the grownup is the ego. The body, intellect, and ego may have grown, but the heart, i.e., such essential qualities as love and compassion, is on its death bed. People think they have become mature adults. But are they really grown up and mature?

"The body has changed from a child's body into a grownup body, but the inner personality is still undeveloped.

"If you continue to cling to the past, you cannot call it maturity. Of course, you can find people with a so-called mature ego, but among them you will not find a truly mature human being. A person with a mature ego may behave in a decent and refined way, but he still acts and speaks in the light of his past. His words and actions in the present are rooted in his past experiences. He has made many mistakes in the past. He has learned a lot from all those experiences; and now, whenever he says or does anything, he is careful not to repeat the same mistakes and not to say something foolish, because he knows from experience that this could create problems. So he chooses his words carefully and acts with deliberation. This shows that the past is still working within him, in a subtle, refined, and powerful way. We may call this maturity, intellectual maturity or maturity of the ego—but it is not real maturity.

"Real, genuine maturity develops when you drop the ego and you stop dwelling in the past. When the inner Self is allowed to express itself, without being tainted or interrupted by the ego, a spontaneous and genuine maturity unfolds."

Question: "Is Amma saying that the growth and maturity of people, which is considered to be so real, is not real at all?"

Mother: "Children, it has a reality of its own. But it is relative. Amma feels that everything should be evaluated from two levels: from a worldly and a spiritual level, from the individual's viewpoint and from a higher perspective, a universal perspective. What seems true from a worldly level may not be real from a spiritual level. The growth and maturity that people generally consider to be real, is not necessarily real from a higher level of consciousness. This doesn't mean that material growth is useless and unimportant. The point is that ordinary human beings consider only proven facts to be real and valid. But the unknown, that which can be known only through faith and constant spiritual practice, coupled with strong determination, is the ultimate Truth and Reality. From that ultimate viewpoint, this world, and what happens in the world, is only relative. Take, for example, the death of a person. As far as his family is concerned, it is certainly a big loss which creates deep sorrow in their lives. But if you look at it from a different angle, there are hundreds of thousands of people dying everyday. Hundreds of thousands of wives are losing their husbands, mothers are losing their children, and children are losing their fathers and mothers. Death must happen to everything that is born—it is inevitable and unavoidable. From a universal level, the death of one person is only relatively real. It is a major and very sad event for the family of the individual, but it is not so from a higher, universal level.

"Similar is the case with growth and maturity. It should be evaluated from both these levels. From the individual's point of view growth of the body and intellect is real and necessary for his existence in the world. But from a universal point of view, real growth happens only when you realize that you are *Purnam* (the Whole), and not an isolated entity, not a part.

"External growth, that is, the growth of the body, mind and intellect, certainly has a place of its own. However, when you are only growing externally, you are not growing fully. As long as the infinite potential of your inner Self remains untapped, your growth is only relative. From the level of the ultimate reality, only when Self-unfolding takes place can we call it real growth.

"Maturity of the ego is necessary for the growth of an individual; this, in turn, will benefit society to a certain extent. But real inner growth and maturity happens only when one transcends the ego, and when the personality grows as a whole. For real, integral growth to take place, the inner Self must unfold. Only then will your vision of life be transformed.

"Humility is the best soil from which the inner Self can unfold. Develop intellectually but always remain humble, then your intellect and maturity will be perfected.

"To be truly humble is to bow down, not just with your body, but with your entire being. You should feel with your whole being that you are nothing, not just before the Master or a few selected souls, but before all of creation. Recognize the Master's supreme consciousness shining in and through everything.

"Grow without allowing your innocence to be destroyed; and as you grow, remain humble in all circumstances. Your

physical growth should not affect the child within. Let your
intellect become sharper, let your mind gain more clarity
and vigor, but along with the development of your faculties,
the feelings of the heart should also be allowed to grow. Such
growth is perfect growth in perfect proportion. It will help
you maintain a healthy and intelligent attitude towards life,
in every possible situation. This verily is the fundamental
foundation of life, which allows you to experience a loving
and intelligent relationship with everyone and everything."

After Mother had finished speaking, one of the devotees
began to sing a song, *Maha Kali Jagado Dharini*, in praise of
Goddess Kali, which he himself had set the tune to. . .

O Mahakali
You sustain the whole universe
And You destroy it
O Giver of solace
You captivate my mind
Please awaken
And cast Your glance on this soul.

O Bearer of salvation
With a necklace of skulls
Giver of boons
O Protector of the three worlds
Destroyer of evil

O Kali!
You captivate my mind
Please awaken
And cast Your glance on this soul.

Brahma, Vishnu and Narada
Are forever worshipping You
Shankara resides forever at Your feet
You are eternally victorious
And untouched by vasanas
You captivate my mind
Please awaken
And cast Your glance on this soul.

At five-thirty in the evening Mother called all the residents to the seashore. By the time everyone arrived at the beach Mother was in deep samadhi. Bri. Gayatri was sitting a few yards away from Her. The residents sat down quietly around Mother. Soon everyone was meditating, except that many of them meditated with open eyes, gazing at Mother. The dark-blue ocean raised its gigantic waves as if to embrace and welcome Mother. The waves seemed to be dancing in bliss at the sight of Mother sitting so close to them on the shore.

An hour later Mother stood up and walked slowly along the beach. It was getting dark and a strong breeze was blowing in from the sea. Mother's white sari and Her curly black hair danced in the wind. The waves seemed to be competing with each other to catch hold of Mother's sacred feet, and to prostrate at those feet. As Mother walked with slow steps along the edge of the ocean, a few waves were fortunate enough to embrace and kiss Her feet. They then peacefully withdrew and merged back into the sea. The other waves chanted loudly the sacred sound, "Aum," and they rushed towards the shore, as if they, too, were hoping to embrace those holy feet.

In a deeply absorbed spiritual mood Mother sang *Omkara Mengum*, as She continued to walk along the shore followed by Her children.

> *The sound 'Om' resonates everywhere*
> *Echoing in every atom.*
> *With a peaceful mind,*
> *Let us chant, 'Om Shakti.'*
>
> *The tears of sadness are overflowing*
> *and now Mother is my only support.*
> *Bless me with Your beautiful hands*
> *For I have given up all worldly*
> *enjoyments,*
> *Sorrowful and worthless as they are.*

The fear of death has disappeared:
The desire for physical beauty is gone.
I must constantly remember Your form
That shines with the Light of Shiva.

When I am filled with an inner light
That overflows and shines before me,
and I am drunk with devotion,
I will merge in the beauty of Your form.

Your form is what I have longed to see
the most
All existing loveliness has crystallized
And come as this unequaled Beauty.
Oh, now my tears are overflowing. . .

When the song ended, Mother stopped walking and stood gazing towards the western horizon for a few more seconds before She turned around and walked back towards the Ashram, followed by the others.

CHAPTER FOUR

"YES, I AM KALI"

few more people and the darshan would be over. Mother ended the darshan and was soon to be found in the dining hall, where She Herself was serving food to all the devotees. Like the most loving and affectionate mother, She waited until everyone had been given their food before She left the dining hall. Just as Mother was leaving, She suddenly turned and approached a visitor. She took a ball of rice, which he had kept aside on his plate, and She ate it without saying a word. As if struck by a thunderbolt the man froze and stared at Mother's face. Tears welled up in his eyes and ran down his cheeks. Soon he was sobbing uncontrollably, calling out, "Kali! Kali!' as he fell at Mother's feet. Stroking his head and back with a radiant, compassionate smile, Mother spent a few more minutes in the dining hall before She returned to Her room.

Later, the man, who came from Bengal, explained the mystery of Mother's seemingly strange behavior and his emotional reaction. He had been in Cochin the previous day, when a friend told him about Mother. Being an ardent devotee of Kali, he felt strongly attracted towards Her. His friend had some urgent work to attend to, so he came to the Ashram alone to meet Mother for the first time. He went up to Mother in the hut and had her darshan. Then later, while sitting in the dining hall in front of the food that had just been served by Mother, he made a ball of rice and put it aside on his plate with the resolve that, "If Mother is Kali, my Beloved Deity, whom I have worshipped for a long time, She will come and eat this rice." So that is what happened. When he saw Mother stepping out of the dining hall, he felt a tremendous sadness. But a moment later Mother was standing in front of him, and before he knew what was happening, Mother took the ball of rice which he had kept aside for Kali and She ate it. The man said, "When Amma ate the rice ball, She was clearly telling me, "Yes, I am Kali." After this incident he was in a divinely intoxicated mood during the entire time he spent in the Ashram, until he left for Calcutta the next morning.

KNOW THE INNER SELF TO BE SELFLESS

This evening, a group of householder devotees came to receive Mother's darshan. Mother was sitting with them behind the old temple.

Whenever Mother is in the midst of Her children, She is more than willing to clear any doubts they may have. When the devotees and brahmacharis are around Mother, their unquenchable thirst for true knowledge takes the form of spontaneous questions. This time a question was asked by a woman who was a college professor, and who had been deeply devoted to Mother for a long time.

Question: "Amma, selfless love and selfless action are considered to be a path to God. But how can one possibly love and act selflessly when one is full of judgment and preconceived ideas? Selflessness sounds more like a goal to be attained, and not something that can be practiced. Amma, could you throw some light on this?"

Mother: "Selfless action is the outward expression of selfless love. When the heart is filled with love, it expresses itself as unselfish action. One is a deep inner feeling and the other its outward manifestation. Without deep, unconditional love, selfless actions cannot be performed.

"In the initial stages, the actions we perform in the name of selflessness are not selfless, because the love that we feel for ourselves is present in everything we do and say; in fact, in the beginning, our self-love is the driving force behind every one of our actions, even though we may call it selfless. Love for the ego, or oneself, is the most predominant feeling in every human being. Unless this feeling dies, real selflessness cannot emerge.

"Alertness is necessary to stop the ego from interfering. It is much easier to be in love with the ego than to feel truly inspired by the ideal of selflessness. Most of the time the selflessness we talk about is really selfish, because everything we do stems from the ego. It is the ego, and not our inner Self, that is the source of our so-called love and our actions. Nothing can be selfless unless it springs directly from the heart, from our true Self. This is the reason why the great saints and sages have said that you should know your own Self before you can love and serve others selflessly. Otherwise, who knows? It could all amount to the fact that you are in love with your own ego, and nothing else.

"Selflessness is the final state to be attained. A person cannot be one hundred percent selfless without getting rid of his preconceived ideas and judgmental attitude. You can, however, have selflessness as your goal, as an ideal, and then try to reach it through the proper methods recommended by the masters.

"There is a story about an old man who was planting mango trees. When his neighbor saw what he was doing, he came to him and said, 'Do you think you will live long enough to taste the mangoes from those trees?'

'No, I doubt it,' replied the old man.

'Then why are you wasting your time?' asked the neighbor.

The old man smiled and said, 'All my life I have enjoyed eating mangoes from trees that have been planted by others. This is my way of expressing my thankfulness to the people who planted those trees.'

"Selflessness can be the driving factor behind all your actions. Learn to be thankful to everyone, to the entire creation, even to your enemy, and to those who insult you and get angry with you, because they all help you to grow. They are mirrors, images of your own mind. If you know how to read and interpret the images properly, you can get rid of your mind and its weaknesses.

"If you choose love and selflessness as your goal, you need to be watchful. Watch your mind constantly, because the mind won't let you do anything selflessly. The mind doesn't want you to be selfless—its one and only aim is to drive you along the path of selfishness, because the mind is selfish. As long as you dwell in the mind you can only be selfish. You have to be free of the mind to be selfless."

WATCH THE MIND

Question: "How, then, does one break out of the mind?"

Mother: "By being watchful and constantly aware. There was a man who used to come to the Ashram. He would criticize everyone and complain about them for hours on end; he never had a good word to say about anyone. Finally, Amma said to him, 'Son, you shouldn't slander people like that. Everyone has weaknesses, but they also have good qualities. Try to see the goodness in everyone. That is the best way to become good in word and deed.' After this he was quiet for a while. But one day when Amma was talking to him, he said, 'Amma, do You know what? Mr. D. says that Mr. S. is a very selfish and unkind man.'

"In one way or another, the mind will keep on playing its tricks. When Amma told this man that he shouldn't criticize others, he couldn't say no to Amma because of his reverence for Her. So he agreed to it outwardly. But deep within he rejected it. His mind just couldn't accept that he should change, because it was such a deep-rooted tendency in him. You see, the mind is a very tricky, wicked thing. His mind didn't want to accept Amma's advice, but at the same time, it wanted to put on a big show, just to impress others. With slight variations and modifications, the mind continued to play its nasty game: 'This man is saying that that man is no good.' See how the mind works!

"So be watchful. Don't let the mind deceive you. It has been playing its tricks and making a fool of you for ages, life after life. To begin with, you need to understand that the mind is a trickster, a clever liar, that stops you from being aware of your true nature, the Self. Constant watchfulness will prevent that liar from lying. You should be so watchful that even if the mind tries to tiptoe through the backdoor, you are immediately aware of it. Nothing should happen without your knowledge; not a single thought or breath should escape without you being aware of it. Once you are able to remain wakeful, keep a close watch on the mind. The mind will then disappear along with the deceptive traps of the past.

SELFLESSNESS IS SPONTANEOUS

"Selflessness is a state of utter spontaneity, which arises once you are established in the Self.

"In the great epic, the *Srimad Bhagavatam*, there is a story about Saint Samika. This story will give you an idea of how spontaneous selflessness can be. King Parikshit, Arjuna's grandson, once went out on a hunting expedition. It was a long and tiring hunt, and the King was eventually overcome by thirst. He went off by himself to find a place where he could get some water. He finally came across the hermitage of Saint Samika. The thirsty and exhausted King entered the hermitage calling out loudly for water. But the Saint was in deep samadhi, oblivious of his surroundings. When Samika didn't respond to the King's repeated request for water, the King became furious. He felt deeply insulted, and losing his discrimination, he picked up a dead snake with the end of his bow and wrapped it around Samika's neck. The King then left the place. But a few young friends of Samika's eight-year-old son, Sringi, witnessed the King's act. They reported the matter to Sringi, who was playing in a nearby field. When the boy was told what had happened, he flew into a rage and he uttered a curse: 'Whoever the person may be who dared to do such a vicious thing to my pure and saintly father, will be bitten by the terrible snake, Takshaka, seven days from now, and will thereby meet his death.'

"Remember that this boy was only eight years old when he uttered the curse. This shows the tremendous willpower that the children, who were brought up in the ancient gurukulas, had in those days. That power was the power of dharma.

"When the Sage came out of his samadhi, he was stunned to learn about the curse that had been uttered against the

King. He immediately fell to his knees and prayed, 'O Lord! My little son, in his ignorance, has committed the unpardonable mistake of cursing a great and just monarch. Please make the curse ineffective and save the King from death.' He summoned his son and sent him to the King's palace to inform him about the curse and to request that the King take the necessary precautions to prevent the curse from being fulfilled.

"The curse, however, could not be reversed. But the great King, Parikshit, only benefited from the curse, because it allowed him to meet the great sage Suka, who told him the stories of the *Bhagavatam*, and thus King Parikshit attained *Moksha* (Liberation).

"The story shows how selfless and forgiving Samika was. He was not at all bothered about the King's lack of discrimination; he didn't feel insulted or abused in any way. When he came to know how the King had wrapped the dead snake around his neck, the Sage said to his son, 'You cursed the King without knowing the truth. The King was thirsty and exhausted. In his desperation, all he could think about was water; and when he couldn't get any, he lost his temper and put the snake around my neck. But, above all, he is the Monarch. Though we live out here in this remote forest, we, too, are his subjects. He protects us; it is thanks to him that we live here safely and undisturbed. Also, the King is a great devotee of the Lord. By cursing him, you will lose the Lord's Grace.'

"Such a beautiful and spontaneous expression of forgiveness can only come from the heart of a selfless soul. Once you are established in the Self, you are egoless, and your selflessness will be spontaneous."

Mother suddenly went into a state of *bhava samadhi*. There was a radiant smile on Her face. She was sitting with Her right hand held in a mudra; her index finger and the little finger were outstretched while the other three fingers were folded together. Inspired by Her divine, intoxicated mood the brahmacharis sang, *Kurirul Pole*. . .

> *Who can that be*
> *With such a terrible form*
> *Dark as the darkest night?*
>
> *Who is that One*
> *Dancing wildly*
> *In this battlefield splashed with blood*
> *Like a bouquet of blue flowers*
> *Twirling in a crimson lake?*
>
> *Who is that One*
> *With three eyes*
> *Flashing like fireballs?*

Who is that One
With thick, black, unfettered locks
Flowing like dark rain clouds?

Why do the three worlds tremble
As Her dancing steps strike the earth?

Oh, that resplendent damsel
Is the sweetheart of Shiva
The Bearer of the trident!

After the song, Mother returned to Her normal mood. The college professor, who was inquisitive and wanted to know more about the attitude of selflessness, asked Mother for further clarification.

Mother: "Before you have attained Realization, whatever actions you do in the name of selfless service are bound to be tainted by selfishness, because everything is filtered through your mind. Only such actions that come straight from the Self and from the heart can be selfless. But don't worry; if you have the determination and the proper attitude, you will eventually become selfless.

"Continue to perform your actions in the world with the attitude of selflessness. In the beginning you have to make a conscious effort to remain intent on the goal. Your conscious effort will in due course become unconscious effort, and this will take you to the state of perfect selflessness. Your selflessness will then be spontaneous. But, for now, you need to be constantly on the watch. The moment the mind interferes, you should be aware of it. Recognize the mind for what it is: an obstacle, the greatest enemy on your path. Know that it is a liar. Ignore the noisy mind and its chattering.

"A medical student is not a doctor. It takes years of concentrated study and preparations to become a good doctor. But during the period when he is still an intern, we might call him a doctor even though he hasn't yet received his degree. Why? Because it is the goal he will reach at the end of his studies. Whatever he does is done as a preparation towards that goal. His aim is to be a doctor; he constantly remembers this and makes every effort to attain that final goal. He refrains from any action or situation that could create an obstacle on his path. Likewise, our final goal is selflessness, but we haven't reached there yet. We do our duty and perform our actions with that state as our goal. Even though our actions at present are not selfless, we call them selfless, in the same way as we might call a medical intern a doctor. But this is still our period of training, and we have a long way to go before getting there. We should be fully intent on the goal; we should avoid any unnecessary thoughts, and whenever we perform an action, we should try to desist from being attached to the action or its fruit. The action is being done now, in this moment—the action is the present, and the fruit is the future. Live in the present moment. Learn to do your actions without any attachment, and ignore the fruit of the future. This attitude will cleanse the mind of all its negativity and impurity, and it will slowly uplift you to the state of selfless love and devotion; it will eventually take you even beyond that, to the ultimate state of Supreme Knowledge.

"You may ask, do we human beings have the capacity to attain the state of love and selflessness? Children, the truth is that human beings alone have the capacity to reach that ultimate state. It depends, however, on how we think and act. This world belongs to us. It is up to us whether we make it heaven or hell. Everything else in nature remains exactly as it is. Only man has the power to choose; and, if he chooses the wrong way, everything will go wrong. He can prepare for himself a bed of poisonous thorns or a bed of divinely scented flowers. Unfortunately, what can be seen around the world is man's hasty preparation of his own deathbed. Consciously or unconsciously, people are moving farther away from true life and closer to death. Even though immortality is readily available, it is being ignored.

"The truth is that death is unnatural to us. Death is natu-

ral only to the body, not to the Self, which is our true being. It is life, the life principle, that is natural. Sorrow is also
unnatural, whereas joy is our natural state. But man seems to
be far more eager to embrace both death and sorrow. He has
forgotten how to smile. Only when you tap into the joy of
the Atman will you truly be able to smile. At the present
stage, however, there is little happiness within, for our hearts
are filled with sorrow; and this is being reflected in every
word, thought and deed. How, then, did this downfall from
immortality take place? Children, it is doubt and fear that
has torn us away from true joy and immortality. However,
that lost, forgotten joy can be regained if we just make the
effort to be selfless. Immortality, which is our true state, can
be rediscovered through the attitude of selfless love and selfless
action.

"One doesn't need any special training to behave selfishly,
because it happens to be the predominant tendency in humans. While all of nature—the birds and the animals, the
mountains, rivers and trees, the sun, the moon and the stars—
stands as a typical example of selfless service, man is the only
one who acts out of utter selfishness and greed. He dwells in
his ego and has made his entire life into a cheap business
venture. For man, there is no longer any sanctity of life; there
is only selfish bargaining. All of life, the entire universe, is

a play of divine consciousness. But man has turned it into a play of the ego.

THE NEGATIVE MIND

"If man wants to be selfish, he doesn't have to be taught, because he is already selfish, except when he is in deep sleep. Even his dreams are selfish, for they are the projections of his selfish mind. Because the mind is inherently negative, so too are most of his dreams. The dream state is a projection of the past. Unless the past disappears, spiritual progress cannot be attained.

"There is a beautiful incident in the *Mahabharata* in which Karna describes the negative and fickle nature of the mind. Karna was revered by everyone for his kindness and his great generosity. One day, he was rubbing oil on his hair as he was preparing for his bath. At that moment Lord Krishna arrived and asked for the jeweled oil cup as a gift. Krishna was testing Karna, for it was reputed that Karna would, without exception, immediately give away whatever was asked of him. He never postponed a chance to give. When Krishna now asked for the jeweled cup that Karna was using, Karna was a bit surprised. He said, 'Ah my Lord, how strange that you should want such a paltry thing. Yet who am I to judge? Here, take it.'—and because Karna's right hand was full of oil, he placed the cup in Krishna's hand with his left hand. But the Lord scolded Karna for offering the gift with his left hand. (In India one would never offer anything with the left hand, as it is considered to be improper.)

'Forgive me Lord!' said Karna. 'As You can see, my right hand is covered with oil and I was afraid that during the time it would take to wash my hand, my untrustworthy mind might change its course and no longer want to give you the cup. My fickle mind would then deprive me of the good fortune obtained by Providence to offer You something. This was why I acted at that very moment. Please forgive me.'

"Children, this is a good description of the mind.

"Amma isn't saying that you should abandon all action, or stop showing any love until you attain the state of Perfection. Your sincere effort to love and to act selflessly must be continued. But Amma wants you to be aware of how subtle the ego is. If you are not constantly watchful and aware, it will trick you by sneaking in through the back door.

"Children, you cannot help anyone without benefiting yourself, nor can you harm anyone without injuring yourself. Listen to this story that Amma heard the other day.

"A man bumped into a friend in the street. When he noticed that his friend was grumbling to himself, he asked, 'What happened? Why are you so upset?'

His friend said, 'That stupid taxi driver at the junction, whenever I meet him, he slaps me on my back. Well, I have decided to show him a piece of my mind!'

His friend cautioned him and said, 'Don't get into trouble.'

But the grumbler insisted, 'This is too much! I have to teach him a lesson!'

'Okay,' said his friend, 'what is your plan?'

'Listen,' said the grumbler, 'today I'm going to hide a stick of dynamite inside my coat; after that he will no longer have an arm to slap me with.'"

Everyone was laughing as Mother finished the story.

Mother continued, "Children, having a selfless attitude will uplift us. By helping others we are, in fact, helping ourselves. On the other hand, every time we do a selfish action, we are harming ourselves. Learn to bless everyone. Don't ever curse anyone, because a human being is not just a bundle of flesh and blood. There is a consciousness at work within everyone. That consciousness is not a separate, isolated entity; it is part of the whole, a Supreme Unity. Whatever we do is reflected in the Whole, in the one Universal Mind— and it returns to you with the same intensity. Whenever you do a good or a bad action, it is reflected in the Universal Consciousness. Therefore, learn to be selfless and learn how to send blessings to everyone. Pray for everyone, because we need the support and blessings of all of Creation for our upliftment.

When we pray for others the entire universe prays for us; and when we bless others the whole universe blesses us, because man is one with the cosmic energy.

"Why did Krishna ask the entire population of Vraja to worship mount Govardhana?[4] He turned that day of worship into a big festival, even though He didn't need anyone's blessings. He did it only to teach humanity the way of seeking, and tapping into, the blessings of all of Creation."

Our beloved Mother Herself sets an example along this line. Before Mother installs the idol during the consecration ceremony of a Brahmasthanam temple, Mother appears in turn, at each of the four doors of the temple, and with joined palms She seeks everyone's permission saying, "The consecration is about to take place. Children, all your blessings are needed." When Mother, who is the infinite power of God in human form, and who can bless the whole of creation with a single glance, seeks the permission and blessings of Her children, it is a unique example of humility. This is a great lesson for us all on how to seek our blessings from everyone and everything, even the most insignificant creature.

---

[4] A sacred mountain near Lord Krishna's birthplace. It is told in the *Srimad Bhagavatam* that He held up the hill on His upraised hand for one week and asked the villagers to take shelter under it from a severe rainstorm.

CHAPTER FIVE

*A*fter holding a program in Kodungallor, Mother and the residents were driving back to the Ashram in the ashram van. When the party reached Alleppy, the van suddenly broke down. Br. Ramakrishnan, who was driving, looked helplessly at Mother. He got out of the vehicle and examined the engine, but there was no obvious problem to be found. He once again tried to start the van but nothing happened. He asked Mother if he should call a mechanic or if they should rent another van. But Mother didn't say anything. She simply smiled, got out of the van and walked away. Ramakrishnan was in a fix. As everyone was walking away with Mother, he followed as well, hoping that She would give him some directions. But Mother ignored his questions. After a few minutes they arrived at the home of Mr. Sekhar whose house was not far from the spot where the van had broken down. Mr. Sekhar and his family were deeply devoted to Mother, and when they saw Mother, they were overjoyed. They laughed and cried at the same time, trying in a panic to quickly get everything organized, so that they could receive Mother in the traditional way. With tears in their eyes they did *pada puja* to Mother, as they chanted a few verses from the *Devi Mahatmyam*.

O Queen of the Universe, You protect the universe. As the Self of the universe, You support the universe. You are the (Goddess) worthy to be adored by the Lord of the universe. Those who bow in devotion to You themselves become the refuge of the universe.

O Devi, be pleased and protect us always from the fear of foes, as You have done just now by the slaughter of asuras. And destroy quickly the sins of all worlds and the great calamities which have sprung from the maturing of evil portents.

O Devi, You who remove the afflictions of the universe, be gracious to us who have bowed to You. O You, worthy of adoration by the dwellers of the three worlds, be a boon-giver to the worlds.

The family had been wanting Mother to visit their home for a long time. They had heard that Mother would return to the Ashram via Alleppy after the Kodungallor program, and they sincerely hoped that Mother would visit their house. Since that morning they had been talking only about Mother, and just a few moments before Mother stepped into their house, Mr. Sekhar and his father were saying to each other that they doubted Mother would visit their house uninvited.

A moment later Mother was standing at the door. They couldn't believe their eyes. It was like a dream.

After the pada puja, Mother went into the family shrine room where She performed *arati*. When the arati was over, Mother called each family member and talked to them individually. She listened to the stories of their aching hearts and affectionately comforted them with Her compassionate touch and with Her soothing words. Mother spent forty-five minutes with the Sekhars.

When Mother left the house, a sad and confused Ramakrishnan was waiting outside. Mother walked back to the ashram van without saying a word. When they reached the vehicle, Ramakrishnan said, "Amma, the van has not been repaired."

Mother got into the van and said, "Try to start it again." Ramakrishnan did as Mother told him and turned the ignition key. The vehicle started immediately and began moving smoothly along the road. With a big grin on his face, Ramakrishnan turned around, looked at Mother and said, "So it was just another one of Your *leelas*!" Mother had a mischievous expression on Her face, as if She were saying, "Son, you have only seen a tiny bit of this infinite leela."

Living with Mother is like being an airplane as it moves on its way to the take-off point. First the airplane moves slowly out of the airdrome towards the runway; it then moves faster and faster along the runway until it finally takes off. If one learns to live in Mother's presence with an attitude of love and self-surrender, it will certainly bring one to the take-off point. In Mother's presence you do not remain the same—you are constantly changing internally. The old patterns disappear as you move deeper and deeper into the new realms of your true existence.

On the way back to the Ashram, Mother visited the homes of two more devotees in Harippad. It was 7:30 p.m. when Mother and the group reached the Ashram. A brahmachari named Anish[5] was waiting for Mother to arrive at the Ashram. He was taking a Vedanta course at another spiritual organization in Bombay. This was his first visit to Mother's Ashram. Mother sat down next to the old temple and talked to Anish while the residents sang the evening bhajans. Those who had been traveling with Mother went and joined the bhajans. They all sang *Akalatta Kovilil. . .*

> *In a distant temple a wick was constantly burning*
> *Guiding those who are groping in the dark.*
> *In this way Mother was showing Her compassion.*

[5] Swami Amritagitananda

One day when I was wandering along that path,
The Radiant One beckoned me with her hand;
She opened the sacred door
Took some holy ash
And rubbed it on my forehead.

She sang the songs of God,
And made a place for me to sleep
With Her own soft hands.
A novel kind of dream then came to me
declaring the truth:
Why do you weep?
Don't you know that you have reached
The sacred feet of the Lord?

I awoke with a sigh
And I clearly saw that Lotus Face
I saw it so clearly.

LOVE AND FREEDOM

After the bhajan everyone quietly watched Mother, who was sitting at the southern side of the temple. One of the brahmacharis spontaneously asked a question.

"Eternal freedom from all bondage is the goal of a true spiritual seeker. But, somehow, there is a misunderstanding concerning this, that the attainment of eternal freedom and the path of love and devotion are two separate things. Amma, kindly throw some light on this."

Mother: "Love and freedom are not two; they are one. They are interdependent. Without love there can be no freedom; and without freedom there can be no love. Eternal freedom can happen only when all your negativity has been uprooted. Only in the state of love will the beautiful, fragrant flower of freedom and supreme bliss unfold its petals and bloom.

"There is an old story about a group of monks who lived in a monastery with their master. The monks led a very devoted and disciplined life. The place had such a wonderful, spiritual atmosphere that people flocked there from far and wide. But one day the master left his body. To begin with, the disciples continued in the same way as they always had; but little by little they began to slacken, their devotion and discipline gradually disappeared, and the monastery fell into a state of neglect. People stopped visiting and no new monks wanted to join the place. All the monks felt deeply discouraged. They often argued with one another, their hearts were dry, and they no longer felt any love or devotion.

"One day, a senior monk decided that something had to be done. He had heard of a spiritual master who lived in a nearby forest. So he left the monastery and went to look for him to seek his advice. When he found the master, he told

him about the neglected state of the monastery and its desperate condition. The master smiled and said, 'There is one
among you who is a great saint, a true incarnation of God
Himself. The residents are not showing him any love or
respect, and that is the cause of all your problems. But the
incarnation of God is living with you in disguise. He will
not reveal his identity.' Having said this, the master closed
his eyes and went into samadhi. The monk could get no more
information out of him.

"On his way back to the monastery, the monk kept
wondering which one among his brothers the Incarnation
could be. 'Could it be the monk who washes our clothes?' he
thought to himself. 'No, it can't be him, for he has too much
of a bad temper. Could it be the cook?' he wondered. 'No, it
can't be the cook because he is far too sloppy in his work
and he doesn't know how to cook good food.' Thus, he went
down the list of all the monks, dismissing each one of them
with some bad quality that he had seen in that monk. But
suddenly he thought to himself, 'It has to be one of the monks,
because the master said so. But I cannot see who it is, because I am only seeing the faults of each one of them; and
what if the Holy One is deliberately showing some fault in
order to better disguise himself?'

"As soon as he reached the monastery, he told his brothers the great news that the master had made known to him. They were all astonished and looked intently at each other, trying to discover who the Incarnation might be (each one knowing it was not himself). But as they looked around they could only see their brothers who they knew so well, with all their faults and blemishes. There was a big discussion among them about who the Incarnation might be. They finally decided to make an effort to respect each other, and to be kind and humble towards each other, because they had no idea who the disguised Mahatma could be, and they didn't want to be disrespectful and arrogant towards him. All the monks agreed that this was an excellent idea. From then on they started treating each other very differently, with great respect and kindness; for they never knew if the monk who stood before them was the Mahatma; and making every effort to see only the goodness in everyone, they began to love each other dearly. Not knowing which one of the monks the Holy One might be, they could not help but imagine they could see Him in every one of their brothers. Through the love that filled their hearts the bondage of negativity which had bound them for so long, dropped away from them. They gradually began to perceive the Holy One clearly, not only in each other, but everywhere—even within themselves, and they attained the state of eternal freedom. The atmosphere of the monastery changed completely, and people began to return there to drink in the love and the divinity that permeated the place.

"So, children, love and freedom are interdependent.

"Complete freedom from the bondage of mind and ego will create a flow of love within. People are bound by the past and the future; that is why it is so difficult to find true love in the world. In order to really be able to love, both the past and the future must dissolve and disappear. You will then experience the present moment as it is; and living this moment in a state of total openness, you then pass on to the next moment, remaining in that same state. When you live in the moment, you are completely here—the next moment doesn't matter to you at all, it never enters your mind. You do not worry about anything, you have no fears or precon- ceived ideas. Similarly, as you continue on to the next moment, you let go of the previous one. The past doesn't matter to you anymore; you forget it. Nothing can bind you—you are ever-free. To truly be able to love, you need to be free of everything. But at the same time, if you are to be completely free, you must have love within. If you are filled with anger, fear or jealousy, you will be a slave to those emotions. Whatever you think, do, or say will be colored by the negativity within you. How can you be free when you are bound by past regrets and by worries about the future? If you, in the name of freedom, try to run away from the world, to a Himalayan cave or to some solitary place, it will only cause you trouble. Your mind will soon feel lonely—and what happens when you are in the grip of loneliness? You languish and begin to dream and brood. Only when we learn to love everyone and everything can we truly be free. Only then will the night of ignorance come to an end and the day of Supreme Realization begin.

"Amma has heard a story. Once a spiritual master questioned his disciples, 'How do you know when the night has ended and the day begun?' A disciple replied, 'When you can see a person at a distance and can tell if it's a man or a woman.' But the master shook his head at the reply. Another aspirant said, 'When you can see a tree standing at a distance and can tell if it's a mango tree or an apple tree. But this answer was also incorrect. The disciples were curious and requested that he enlighten them by giving the correct answer. The master smiled and said, 'When you behold your brother in every man, and your sister in every woman, then the night has ended and the day begun. Until that time, even when the sun illumines the earth at the height of noon, it is still night and you are in the dark.'

"Children, this is a good story to remember. Only when

you learn to love everyone equally will true freedom emerge. Until then, you are bound; you are the slave of your mind and ego.

"So, in order to be free you have to love. But also, to be able to love selflessly you should be free of everything that binds you, both physically and mentally."

LIVE ACCORDING TO YOUR OWN DHARMA

A householder devotee raised a question.

"Amma, we are family people who have to work in the world to earn our livelihood and to protect our families. Do we have to choose any particular field of action to experience this love and freedom?"

Mother: "Children, stay where you are and do your duty with love and dedication. If you are married and settled in the world, don't run away, abandoning your job and your responsibilities as a husband or wife, and parent. Don't think that God will accept you only if you renounce all your duties and wear ochre-colored clothes. No, that is not how it is. Continue to wear the same clothes, perform your duties, stay at home and do your work. But at the same time, learn to live within your true Self. This is the most important art that we should learn. We learn everything else but never this: the art of being in our own Self.

"We should try to live according to our own dharma. We should never try to adopt someone else's dharma, for that would be as dangerous as it would be if a dentist were to act as a cardiologist and treat someone afflicted with heart disease. It would be dangerous for both him and his patients if he tried to do something which he is not qualified to do. Needless to say, the dentist should stick to his own job. He has enough to do in his own field. By diligently performing each action with an attitude of love, dedication, and self-surrender, he can attain perfection."

A devotee remarked, "In the *Srimad Bhagavad Gita* it is written: 'Better to die in one's own duty; the duty of another is fraught with danger.'" (*Ch.3, v.35*)

Mother smiled and continued, "One cannot live without being active in some way, whether physically, mentally, or intellectually. Everyone is constantly engaged in some form of action; this is an unchangeable law of nature. No one becomes pure and selfless overnight; it involves time and concentrated effort coupled with tremendous patience and love. Do your actions in the world, without forgetting that your final goal in life is to break out of all bondage and limitations. Always remember that you have a higher goal to attain. Simply do what needs to be done; but at the same time, don't miss the opportunities you come across to perform unselfish actions. You will then gradually gain mental purity and devotion. As you proceed with diligence, you will attain more clarity of mind and a deeper understanding. This will finally lead you to the state of Perfection, the state of Self-Realization.

"Any action done with the right attitude, understanding, and discrimination will take you closer to liberation. If, however, the same action is done without the right attitude, it will bind you. An action can either serve as a purifier, which will finally help you realize your godly nature, or it may add more and more to the already existing amount of negativity, which will eventually cause you tremendous suffering.

"Whenever you are doing something, try to be aware. If you are constantly watchful, you will slowly begin to take notice of the unnecessary burden of negative thoughts you are carrying. Watchfulness helps you to drop all your burdens and to be free.

"Nothing should happen without your knowledge. Not even a single thought should go by without you being aware of it. Closely observe the mind and its different moods. As you consciously observe, you can clearly see what is happening within you. If you are watchful when anger arises, it cannot escape without your knowledge. But observation alone is not sufficient. Try to find the root cause of a particular mood such as anger."

HOW TO TRACE AND UPROOT ANGER

Question: "Amma, how does one trace the cause of anger and uproot it?"

Mother: "Something has caused that anger; there must be a root cause that triggers it off. That cause is invisible. You have to search for that invisible root within. The anger is at the surface, which is why you can see it through close intro- spection. But now you have to look for the root cause which lies hidden in your subconscious, deep beneath the surface of the mind. Only by uprooting that cause can you destroy the anger that is creating all the turbulence on the surface.

"The anger at the surface of the mind can be compared to a tree. The cause of the anger is like the unseen root of the tree lying hidden beneath the soil. All the strength of the tree is derived from the root. If you want to destroy the tree, you just have to uproot it. Once the root is destroyed, the tree will automatically die. In a similar way, once you become aware of the negativity within you, you should practice introspection and search for the root of that negativity. Just as the tree exists because of the root, the negativity within you, whatever it may be, exists because of its powerful cause lying deep within the mind. Investigate and find that root. As you discover the cause behind the negativity, it disappears, never to come back again. This is possible only by being watchful.

"When you are watchful, you cannot move in the wrong direction, nor can you do anything unrighteous. Constant watchfulness makes you so pure, that at last, you yourself become the very embodiment of Purity—and that is your true being. Once you reach this highest state, your every intention, word and action, becomes pure. The burden of impurity is no longer there. The light of purity is all that exists. You then behold everything as Pure Consciousness. This means that you see everything as equal. External appearances are no longer significant, for you have developed the ability to penetrate deeply and to see through everything. Matter, which is ever-changing, loses its importance. Within everything you see only the immutable Atman (Self)."

Mother closed Her eyes and began to sing *Santamayi Orukatte. . .*

> Let the River of Life glide along gaily
> To join at last
> the Infinite Ocean of Silence,
> To merge into the
> Ocean of Sat, Chit, Ananda.

The seawater evaporates
massing into swollen clouds,
Which again rain down
to become flowing rivers,
Rushing, hurrying to empty into the ocean.

Our experiences, though varied,
have a purpose in the Divine Play,
Our life, running in windy ways,
is goaded by an urge
To lose and fulfill itself
in the Great Beyond, the Divine.

The River of Life thus flows on and on,
Deepening in experience and wisdom;
Let it glide on smoothly, without a hitch,
For the final tryst with its Lord.

Mother is the embodiment of Supreme Purity and Love. In Her presence purification happens effortlessly. In that Purity, the entire universe is reflected and the cosmic energy experienced. To this Supreme Light, Purity and Love we can offer ourselves, and we will be made pure in return. Mother will happily accept our impurity in exchange for the purity and love She bestows upon us. Approach Her with the prayer, "O Mother, here is Your child! I am incapable of offering You anything but my impurity. O great Giver of everything, receive my life. Purify me, and let me be a pure instrument of Yours, forever."

ASK YOURSELF,
WHY CAN'T I JUST SMILE AND BE HAPPY?

An American devotee said to Mother, "Mother, my past is bothering me terribly. Is there no way to escape? You tell me to smile but I cannot smile. I feel so tense and frightened. What can I do to overcome this and begin to smile, as you are telling me to do?"

Mother replied, "Daughter, as long as you are carrying the burden of your past, you cannot genuinely smile. You have to ask yourself, 'Why am I sad? Why can't I just smile and be happy?'

"Look at the beauty and perfection of nature. Everything in nature is so joyful, even though it doesn't have the intelligence of a human being. All of creation is rejoicing. The most beautiful flowers are picked by people—torn by their stems. Some are made into garlands while others are trampled. A flower has such a short life span, and yet it offers itself wholeheartedly to others; it even offers its own nectar to the bees—and yet it is happy. The stars are twinkling in the sky, the rivers are flowing blissfully, the branches of the trees are dancing in the wind, and the birds are bursting into song. You should ask yourself, 'Why, then, do I feel so miserable living in the midst of all this joyful celebration?'

"Ask the question, 'why,' repeatedly, and you will find the answer. The answer is that the flowers, stars, rivers, trees, and birds do not have an ego; and, being egoless, nothing can hurt them. When you are egoless, you can only rejoice. Even occasions which normally would be painful, are transformed into moments of joy.

"But unfortunately, you have an ego, and you have been wounded by people many times. There is a mountain of hurt feelings within you. Your individuality, your ego, has been hurt. All those wounds are in bad shape: pus and blood is oozing out. It is amazing that you choose to live in that state without finding an effective cure.

"As mentioned earlier, the best cure is to closely observe the mind. This will bring the hidden cause of your suffering into light. The ego is the cause, the invisible root. The invisible but powerful ego needs to be exposed. Just by being exposed the ego disappears, saying, "I have nothing to do here, so good-bye—I will never see you again.' It won't say, 'See you later.' Exposing the ego is the same as destroying it; it is like exposing a thief in his hideout.

"Drop all your regrets of the past and relax. Relaxation

will help you acquire more strength and vitality. Relaxation is a technique through which you can catch a glimpse of your real nature, the infinite power source of your existence. Learn to be relaxed during times of stress and strain. Learn to stand aside and just watch the negative thoughts, the hurt feelings and the mental agony you are going through. As this happens, withdraw your cooperation and your involvement with the stress and the agony. Once you learn this technique, you will realize that the tension, burdens, and negativity you are carrying belong to the mind; they don't belong to the inner Self, your true being.

"You may not experience total relaxation in the beginning, you may get only a hint of it at first; but once you get a taste, you become interested. It is a wonderful experience which you relish; you want to experience it again and again, in ever increasing amounts. As you learn the technique of entering into that mood, you become immensely desirous of remaining in that state, because for a moment you are able to forget everything; for a few seconds you have experienced real peace and joy, and you cannot let go of those precious moments. Also, the vibrant wakefulness you experience after that moment of relaxation is indescribable. You feel an unquenchable thirst to return to that state.

"Remember: relaxation gives you the strength and en-

ergy to confront the challenges awaiting you in the future.
Just be at ease and, at the same time, be watchful."

Mother asked the brahmacharis to sing a bhajan. They
sang together, *Anantamayi Patarunnor...*

> *The vast, expanding sky*
> *The inner Being*
> *Vibrant with enthusiasm*
> *Awakens!*
> *O Mother!*
> *Goddess Ambika, Eternal Virgin,*
> *Infinite, Blissful and Immaculate. . .*
>
> *Never—O, never again allow*
> *this suppliant*
> *To succumb to temptation!*
> *As the days go by*
> *The pain of my heart increases;*
> *O Goddess of my heart,*
> *Aren't You aware of it?*
>
> *Don't I have a Mother?*
> *Is there no Mother for me?*
> *Tell me, O Blissful One*
> *Tell me. . .*
> *I do not seek bliss or anything else*
> *Give me only pure love and devotion.*

WATCHFULNESS AND SHRADDHA

When the song came to an end, everyone sat in silence for some time until another question was asked.

"Amma, is watchfulness the same as *shraddha?*"

Mother: "Children, the whole of spirituality can be put into one word, and that is 'shraddha.' Shraddha is the unconditional faith the disciple has in the words of the Master or in the scriptural dictums. The Master's words are in full accord with the words of the scriptures. In fact, a true Master's words are verily the scriptures. A disciple who is endowed with such faith will be constantly watchful of his mind and thoughts. So in that sense shraddha is also watchfulness. The meaning of shraddha is to be constantly aware. But this is only possible when you are relaxed. A tense, agitated person, who is constantly thinking about his failures in life, cannot be watchful, nor can he be fully aware of the present moment. It is the same with a person who keeps dreaming about the future. Both of these moods will make you inert; you lose your creativity and cannot be productive. Relaxation, however, will enhance your awareness and bring out your real being. Only a relaxed person can be ever watchful and aware.

"Children, failures are bound to happen in life. Suppose we have stumbled over something and fallen. We don't say to ourselves, 'Okay! Now that I've fallen, let me remain lying here on the ground forever. I'm not going to get up and proceed to my destination.' It would be ridiculous to think like that.

"A toddling child will fall countless times before he can walk properly. Similarly, failures are a natural part of life. Keep in mind that each failure comes with the message of success. Just as a toddler will fall before he or she learns to walk with firm steps, our own failures are the beginning of our ascent towards ultimate victory. So there is no need to feel disappointed or frustrated. Don't remain in the dark. Come out into the light.

YOU ARE THE LIGHT OF GOD

"You don't belong to the dark. The darkness is a prison created by your own mind and ego; it is self-imposed and self-created. It is not your real abode, for you belong to the light. You are the light of God. So let go of the dark. Realize that you are in prison; recognize the prison for what it is, and understand that it is not your real home. We have created our own prison and our own imprisonment. Nobody else is responsible or involved. Observe that the darkness is dark, and not light. We are in the dark but unfortunately we think we are in the light. Thinking is the problem. We are totally identified with the thought process.

"In our present mental state, although we are in the dark and are bound by the self-created ego, we believe that we are free and in the light. We are mistaking darkness for light, and bondage for freedom. It is a question of recognizing the bondage for what it is. We don't understand that we are chained, for we have been in chains, in the dark, for a long time. The chains that bind us are like ornaments to us, and the prison has become almost like a home. What we consider to be embellishments—fame, power, wealth—are, in fact, the chains that bind us. Because of this mistaken concept, misery and sadness have become part of our lives, and this is why we cannot smile wholeheartedly. But the truth is the opposite. We are the light of the Divine, and bliss is our birthright. We are the eternally free, infinite Atman.

"There is a vague memory of our true nature within us. Sometimes this memory becomes a little clearer. But most of the time we are unaware of it, which is why we continue to remain in bondage. Whenever the memory stirs, we struggle to free ourselves. This chain, however, is such that the more you struggle, the tighter it becomes. Stop struggling, quiet down and relax, and you will discover that you are free. Being aware of the bondage is enough to free you from its clutches.

You are holding on to all the illusory objects created by the mind. You unwisely identify with your thoughts, thus creating your own prison and being imprisoned therein. How do you free yourself? It is very simple. Just release the grip and withdraw your cooperation—just let go.

"Do you know how monkeys are caught in some parts of India? A narrow-necked pot, filled with nuts and other eatables that monkeys like, is placed on the ground. Then a monkey comes to take the nuts. He puts his hand into the pot and grabs hold of the nuts. Now, because his hand is full he cannot take it out of the narrow-necked pot. The foolish monkey doesn't open his hand and let go of the nuts, which would be an easy way to escape. He won't let go of the nuts he has grabbed, and so he is trapped. By holding on to a few nuts, the poor monkey loses the entire forest with all its beautiful trees—the vast area where he could roam freely, play and enjoy life to his heart's content. Just for the sake of a few nuts he loses the abundance of fresh and delicious nuts and fruits available throughout the forest. He loses his entire world.

"Human beings are much the same. A person calls out, 'Free me! I want freedom!' But who has chained him? What is binding him? No one—nothing. He just has to stop creating all this unnecessary noise, stop struggling, calm down and relax; then he will see that it is he, and he alone, who is responsible for his own bondage. He just has to let go of the few nuts he is holding onto, and he can then easily take his hand out of the narrow-necked pot of body, mind, and intellect. He can be ever-free. The entire universe belongs to him."

CONSOLING A DISTRESSED SOUL

A woman devotee from the West was sitting next to Mother looking very sad. Mother turned to her and lovingly asked her what was troubling her. The woman looked at Mother with tears in her eyes. She seemed to want to have a private conversation with Mother. With a sign of Her hand Mother asked everyone to leave, except Bri. Gayatri who was needed as a translator. The woman then opened Her heart to Mother. She had had two abortions in the past, and she was constantly in deep agony thinking about it. The woman told Mother, "The more I try to forget, the stronger it becomes. I cannot forgive myself. Mother, forgive me for what I have done! Help me to forget and to be at peace."

Mother looked at her with great compassion and gently rubbed her chest. She consoled her saying, "Daughter, don't think that what you have done is a great sin. It was the karma of both you and the two children to go through that experience. The fetuses were destined to live only for that long. Now that you have met Amma you should forget about it. Don't react to the past. There is force and aggression implied in reaction. Reaction creates more turbulence in the mind and the very thought you are trying to forget will come up with much more strength. To react is to fight. Fighting the wounds of the past will only deepen those wounds. Relaxation is the method that heals the wounds of the mind, not reaction.

"The mere realization of your wrongdoing has freed you from it. You have already been forgiven. The pain you have suffered is more than enough to wash away the sin. Any sin will be washed away by the tears of repentance. Daughter, Amma knows that you have suffered alot. From now on you shouldn't carry this burden in your mind. You have Amma to take care of you. Forget it and be at peace."

Those nectarous words of Mother's made the woman break down in tears. Mother gently put Her arms around the woman and drew her onto Her lap. The woman lay with her head on Mother's lap and continued to weep. As Mother caressed the woman's hair She said to Gayatri, "Poor woman! She committed those acts out of ignorance. At the time She must have found herself in very difficult circumstances, which was why she destroyed the child. Her guilty conscience has haunted her during all these years."

A few brahmacharis had been lingering at a distance, unable to completely pull themselves away from Mother's presence. Mother called them back, and they all came and sat down in front of Her. The woman continued to rest her head on Mother's lap as Mother spoke and Gayatri continued to translate.

NO ONE SHOULD BE PUNISHED ETERNALLY

"Whatever may be the gravity of the mistake you have committed, once you realize your mistake and feel remorseful, you need to be forgiven. This does not mean that anyone can consciously commit a mistake and think they will be free from punishment, as long as they repent later. No, that is not the case. As far as possible, we should refrain from making any mistakes. As mortal human beings, we are bound to make mistakes, sometimes out of ignorance, at other times due to the pressure of our circumstances. As a lesson, a certain amount of punishment may be necessary, depending on the seriousness of the mistake. Punishment is definitely necessary if a person consciously keeps committing the same mistakes, again and again. However, nobody should have to suffer forever; no soul should be punished eternally because of a few mistakes he has committed or has intended to commit.

There are some people who sincerely regret their sins. They realize what they have done and wish to change. They should be given every opportunity to start afresh with a new out-look on life. They should be forgiven; a conducive and lov-ing environment should be created around them, so that they can forget and let go of the past, and live fully productive lives. They need your love and compassion. Smile at them from your heart and speak to them lovingly. Let your en-couraging words and your smile touch their hearts and heal their wounds. If you can touch them with your love and compassion, they will be able to let go of the darkness of their past. Because of your compassion they will feel that they are loved; they will begin to relax and be at peace with themselves. Don't ever reject them or call them sinners; for, in that case, not only they, but all of us are sinners, for we have all committed the great mistake of forgetting our true nature, our existence in God. No mistake can be greater than this, for which we could all be punished. But God is all-compassionate and all-forgiving. God has forgiven us. Amma doesn't believe that God will let any soul suffer forever. If He did, He wouldn't be God."

With the woman still resting on Her lap, Mother began to sing, *Amme Yi Jivende. . .*

O Mother of the Universe,
There is no one but You
Who can wipe the tears from this face
And liberate my soul.
Upon reaching Your feet,
This soul realizes itself.

Alas!
Even now, this mind is steeped in sorrow
For it has lost its way in Maya
before reaching the goal.
Please bless me
That I may hold You forever
With pure devotion
In a tight embrace.

In this fearsome ocean of birth and death
The only refuge is Your Lotus Feet.
Won't You come
And sprinkle a little nectar of Love
On this smoldering one?

This little infant spends every moment
Meditating on Your form;
Please don't let me wait any longer;
Draw me close to You
Bestow inner peace
On this tortured soul.

At the end of the song, Mother gently made the woman sit up. The woman looked as if a heavy load had been lifted away from her. Her face was brighter and she smiled happily at Mother. Letting out a deep sigh she said, "Ah, Mother, I feel so peaceful now. You have brought light into the dark chamber of my heart. Thank You so much!"

Mother stood up, gave the woman another hug, and walked away towards the edge of the backwaters.

CHAPTER SIX

RESPECT WITHOUT LOVE CREATES FEAR

*M*other was sitting outside the old kitchen in the midst of the brahmacharinis and householders, cutting vegetables. Sensing that Mother was there, a few more brahmacharinis arrived within a few minutes. As the vegetable chopping progressed Mother noticed that one of the girls was peeling too much of the skin from a cucumber. Mother said, "Daughter, why do you remove that much? Don't waste anything unnecessarily. Only a person who has no shraddha will waste things. Whatever actions a spiritual seeker performs must be well thought out. We should be able to transmit the silence and the stillness that we gain through our meditation into our actions. In fact, meditation helps one to gain a deeper insight into all the aspects of one's actions. Once this depth is attained, you won't waste anything unnecessarily. By peeling away too much of the skin you are removing some of the edible part as well. This means that you are denying the benefit of it to everybody in the Ashram, as well as to others, including those who are starving and who would really benefit from it. A person who has gained a certain amount of inner silence and stillness through meditation and other spiritual practices will never do such things."

Mother paused and a question was asked.

"Amma, I heard you say once that a disciple should feel both love and respect towards the Master. You also said that if there is only respect, there is bound to be fear. Could you please explain this?"

Mother: "When there is only respect and no love, fear is bound to occur. There is an aspect of fear in respect. The school teacher asks the student to learn a poem by heart before he comes to class the next day. The poor student isn't interested in poetry. He'd rather play sports and watch TV. The student respects his teacher, but he doesn't love him. He feels that the teacher is forcing something on him that he doesn't like. He dare not say no to his teacher, because he is afraid of him and also of his parents, and of the punishment he may get if he doesn't obey. So he repeats the poem several times and learns it. This is not real learning. No real learning is possible as long as there is fear. This form of learning will never help the student to attain any true knowledge, because it isn't done with the heart. Out of respect and fear of his teacher, the student learns like a parrot without imbibing the meaning. But the student's heart is closed. Fear

closes the heart and there is then every probability that the
student will forget what he has learned. Only if the heart is
open, can he really learn. Otherwise, the process of learning
and all his actions will be mechanical.

"You feed information into a computer and you store the
information there. Whenever you want to use this information, you simply press a few keys and it appears before you.
But, if you happen to press the wrong button by mistake,
that's it!—all the data you have saved is gone. The screen
goes blank.

"The computer can only obey whatever command it is
given. The computer is not intelligent and it cannot feel
anything, because it's only a machine invented by the human intellect.

"A human being can become almost like a breathing,
moving computer, if he doesn't have a loving and compassionate heart. Respect that is devoid of love and based on
fear, will close your heart and turn you into a human machine. If you obey your teacher or your parents only out of
fear and respect, it is no more than feeding information into
a computer. It can go blank at any time, because there is no
love to hold and support it.

"The other day a family came to see Amma. They had a
seven-year old son. He was sitting on Amma's lap, and just

to make him happy and to make him talk, Amma asked him several questions: his name, what grade he was in, about his friends, the games he liked, etc. Each time he was about to answer a question, the boy would first look at his father, as if asking permission to speak. The boy would answer each question only after being given his father's consent. When Amma asked what his name was, he immediately looked at his father. Only when his father said, 'Tell Amma your name,' did the boy dare say his name. The boy was afraid to speak. You cannot even call this respect—it is plain fear. If you threaten a child saying, 'Obey, or I will punish you,' you don't know how much harm you are doing. The child closes up and cannot express himself. He will carry this fear within him throughout his life. He may become a wealthy man, highly educated, holding a top position in society, but the fear will still be there, deep within him, and it will make his personal life a living hell.

"Creating fear and respect in order to teach obedience cannot be called disciplining, which is what we like to call it. True, constructive disciplining takes place when love is allowed to blossom. If love is absent, any reverence or re-spect will be based on fear. A loving relationship, however, will open up your heart and enable you to express yourself fully in whichever way you choose. Love brings you closer together, and in that closeness there is no lack of discipline at all. Out of that love, which comes from proper understanding, a natural and genuine respect will be born. In other words, once a strong bond of love is established between the teacher and student, or parent and child, disciplining can be done easily, without causing any hurt feelings in the one who is being disciplined. This loving closeness, this meeting of hearts, is vitally important in the relationship between parent and child, or teacher and student. But for this closeness to happen, one must be patient and forgiving.

"Children, you might have heard about the Guru-disciple relationship that existed long ago. Students from all different casts and backgrounds used to come and stay at the gurukula. The period of education would last for at least twelve years. The system was entirely different in those days. It was not at all like modern schools and colleges. Nowadays, the students cannot study without writing notes and staring at their textbooks. During class the students barely ever look at the face of their teacher; they are either writing notes, sitting hunched over their textbooks, or daydreaming through the window. They don't look at their teacher's face, because they don't like his face. The students feel resentful towards their teacher. Outwardly, they may be respectful towards him, but deep within they resent him. Respect without love is usually born out of fear, which, in turn, may culminate in anger and even hatred.

"Most children feel some resentment towards their fathers and teachers, because they are being controlled by them. They feel that the adults are trying to impose their own ideas upon them. As long as a youngster is still dependent on his father and teachers, he isn't in a position to express his anger. Some children, of course, erupt and cause problems, but the majority lie low during their period of dependency. They are instinctively concerned about their own security. However, once they are free of their dependency, they often explode and begin to vent their feelings. The child or student keeps his anger suppressed in his subconscious. During his period of dependency he may mask his anger in an outward show of love and respect, because he needs his father and teacher; he needs their material support and education. But once that period is over, he cannot suppress his anger any longer, and it comes out. Thoughts such as, 'He controlled me, he didn't do what I wanted, he punished me and insulted me in front of everyone," may manifest as anger and even hatred. He then wants to take revenge. All his respect disappears, because the respect was never real; it wasn't rooted in love. He now reveals the real face hidden behind the mask of respect: the face of anger. This happens in all such relationships if the proper love and understanding is absent. It is only a question of time. The anger keeps smoldering within until a situation arises which causes it to flare up. Until then, if the individual, who is involved in any type of relationship, doesn't cultivate the right attitude with the proper love and understanding, he will be carrying a hidden volcano within. This is the experience of hundreds of thousands of people. Because of Her personal contact with the millions of people She has met from all walks of life around the world, Amma can assure you that this is true. Of course, there are exceptions; there are people who lead happy and well balanced lives, but the majority fall under the above said category."

Mother stopped for a while and asked the brahmacharis to sing a song. They sang *Amritanandamayi Janani. . .*

> *Mother Amritanandamayi*
> *You are the embodiment of mercy*
> *Compassion, wisdom and bliss.*
>
> *You are the remover of all obstacles*
> *The Mother of Vinayaka Ganesha.*
> *O Mother*
> *You are the embodiment of holiness*
> *And of knowledge*
> *You are the bestower of intellect*
> *The Vedas are Your form*

You are Consciousness and the Pure Self
O Mother Amritanandamayi.

Amritanandamayi
You are Saraswati, the Goddess of Knowledge
With the book and the veena in Your hands
You are Brahman
You are Mahalakshmi, the Goddess of Wealth
Parvati, the Goddess of Power
Sankari, the Auspicious One
And Adi Parashakti, the Primordial Power.

You are Vishnumayi
The dynamic Power of the Sustainer,
And Shiva-Shakti
The Active and the Passive.
Mother of the universe
Please protect us!
Appear to us in Krishna- and Devi Bhava
O Amritanandamayi. . .

Mother's eyes were closed. The brahmacharis sat in silence around Mother, gazing at Her and trying to absorb the profound meaning of the song they had just sung. After a few minutes Mother opened Her eyes and smiled at Her children. One of the brahmacharis said, "Amma, kindly enlighten us by saying something more about the Guru-sishya relationship which existed in the ancient gurukulas."

THE GURU-SISHYA RELATIONSHIP
IN THE ANCIENT GURUKULA

Mother: "In the *gurukulas* of the ancient rishis, where the disciples lived with a Master, serving him and studying their lessons, there was no such thing as students writing notes or sitting in class with their heads plunged into textbooks. The disciples simply sat gazing at the Master as he spoke. That was all. There were no notes or textbooks. Whatever the Master said went straight to their hearts. This was possible because of the deep bond that had been forged between the Master and his disciples. The Master's way of disciplining his disciples was not done unwisely in a forcing or control-ling way; on the contrary, it was a relationship born out of true love and understanding. The Master truly cared for his disciples and they in turn showed their love and respect by caring deeply for him. It was not respect born out of fear, but out of deep love.

"The Master opened the door of his heart to his disciples. He welcomed and accepted them wholeheartedly without any reservations. The Master's openness and selflessness made the disciples receptive and humble in his presence. Even though the Master was a treasure chest of knowledge, he was also very humble. He didn't have the attitude that, 'I am the master and you are my disciples, so you'd better do whatever I say, or I'll punish you.' The disciples were free to ask the Master any questions if they needed to clear their doubts. Because the Master was the embodiment of knowledge he could dispel their doubts both through theory and practice. In the modern classroom even if the students have doubts and questions they hesitate to ask anything, because of the lack of love and closeness between them and their teacher. Neither teacher nor students are open enough or thirsting to give or receive any real knowledge. Both teacher and students are arrogant. The teachers find it difficult to clear all the doubts of their students, because they themselves never imbibed any real knowledge when they were students. Their relationships with their teachers were similarly lacking.

"In the ancient gurukula, the Master prayed together with his disciples: 'May Brahman protect us, may He nourish both you and I, may both you and I be given the energy we need, may this study make us both illumined, and may we never hate each other. Om shanti, shanti, shanti.' The prayer was dedicated to both teacher and students, blessing each one's uplift and understanding—not that the master needed anything from the disciple—it was only a magnificent example of his humility.

"The Master was always in a prayerful mood. You know, children, a person who is constantly in a state of prayer cannot be egotistic. He is humble in all circumstances. In those days, humility, love and patience were the factors that made people's lives so beautiful and complete. Even though the Master was fully enlightened and all-knowing, he was still humble in front of his disciples.

"No one can feel egotistic in front of a genuinely humble soul. So the disciples who came to study with such a Master, even though they weren't free from the ego, turned out to be humble and obedient in his presence. In those days, royal princes, the children of noblemen, and students who belonged to all the different classes of society, came to the Master's gurukula. But to the Master they were all the same. They lived together, ate and slept together, and were all taught the same lessons. They had to do physical work, including looking after the Master's cows, fetching firewood from the forest, taking care of the crops and so on. But still, there was tremendous love between the Master and his disciples. There was not a trace of anger or resentment.

"When there is that much love, your heart is wide open, as open as that of a child. It was this openness, born out of love, that helped the disciples to learn by simply listening to the Master and gazing at his face. They never needed to write notes or to use a textbook, nor did they have to repeat a poem or an essay a hundred times to learn it. They listened once to the Master, and that was enough: they remembered it till the end of their lives. They never forgot what they had learned while gazing at the face of their beloved Master. Real listening happens only where there is love.

"When the Master spoke it was Love that spoke; and at the receiving end it was absorbed by nothing but Love. Because of their love for their Master, the heart of each disciple was like a fertile field, ready to receive the knowledge imparted by the Master. Love gave and love received. Love made them open to each other. True giving and receiving takes place where love is present. Real listening and shraddha is possible only where there is love, otherwise the listener will be closed. If you are closed, you will be easily dominated by anger (your past) and resentment, and nothing can enter into you."

THE MODERN EDUCATIONAL SYSTEM AND THE ANCIENT WAY OF A TRUE MASTER

Question: "What is the problem with the modern educational system?"

Mother: "In the modern educational system this openness is absent. Both teacher and student are closed to each other.

There is no sharing and no love; there is only resentment. The teachers are not humble, and many are arrogant. They want to control the students and to force their own ideas upon them. If the students don't listen, the teachers get angry and want to punish them. Due to their unintelligent way of approaching the students, the teachers in modern schools and colleges shut off any possibility of establishing a loving relationship with the students, and to thereby help them dive into the depths of true knowledge. One of the most important reasons for the degeneration of the educational system is this absence of a loving bond, of a positive relationship which could bring the teacher and student closer to each other. Only a flow of genuine love and acceptance from both sides could make them understand each other, which in turn would open up the gates between them for true sharing to happen.

"But they are poles apart, and this inner distance makes learning impossible. Their egos have created a big gulf between them. The teacher is speaking, not with love, but with the proud feeling that, 'I am the teacher and you are my student. I know everything and you know nothing, so you'd better listen to me, or else. . .' The student feels this pride. He, too, is proud, and when he senses the pride in his teacher he thinks, 'Why should I listen to that fellow? I'm not going to!' His heart is closed and now there is a big wall between them. The teacher continues to speak but nothing reaches the student. Physically the student is present in the class-room and the teacher is standing just a few yards away, but in reality, they are very far away from each other. Both of them are closed. When a closed heart speaks, nothing comes out; the knowledge only echoes within the speaker; it can-not create any impact at the other end—a closed heart speaks and a closed heart listens. In other words, no real imparting of knowledge takes place.

"Everybody craves attention in the modern age, because attention is food for the ego. The ego lives on attention. Both the teacher and student strongly crave attention, and if it isn't forthcoming, their minds become filled with anger and revenge. There are even instances when students and teachers seriously hurt each other.

"The kind of teacher-student relationship that we have today cannot transform a person or help anyone grow. No real knowledge will dawn within the student in this way. It will only create negative feelings in both teacher and stu-dent. As you carry around the burden of unhealed wounds that have been caused by such incidents, your whole life becomes a wound, infected with the pus of your intense negative feelings.

"There was a time when a Master would transform his disciples by his mere presence; or, it would be more appropriate to say that the transformation just happened to the disciples. Such was the power of the Master's presence.

"The power that created this transformation was the love and compassion the disciples experienced in their Master's presence. When someone's heart is filled with love and compassion, your own heart will spontaneously open up like a blossoming flower. The closed bud of your heart unfolds in the presence of love. The Master doesn't necessarily give you any instructions as such, he may not teach you verbally—the opening up simply happens, as naturally as a flower opens up its petals. This is bound to happen in the presence of a true Master.

"A flower doesn't need instructions on how to bloom. No music teacher taught the nightingale to sing. It is spontaneous. There is no force involved, it happens naturally. Similarly, in the presence of a great Master, the closed bud of your heart opens up. You become as receptive and innocent as a child, a humble and obedient child of the Master. He doesn't teach you anything. You learn everything without being taught. His presence, his very life, is the greatest teaching of all. There is no control or force involved; everything happens naturally and effortlessly. Only love can create this miracle.

"In the modern educational system the students are being drained of their energy, by having to repeat the lessons countless times in order to memorize them. Education has become an energy dissipating process. The students are constantly under great pressure; and the stress and strain caused by their parents, especially during examination time, is often noticeable.

"Amma is saying that whether one's goal is spiritual or material, nothing can be achieved if there is too much pressure coming from all directions.

"The modern educational system lies like a heavy, overloaded sack on the student's shoulders, and the parents often make it worse. The parents have only one mantra which they incessantly repeat to their children: 'You should study your lessons, do your homework and do nothing but study.' During examination time the students are under great pressure. They are not relaxed at all.

"Teach them the art of relaxation, how to be at ease. If they don't feel relaxed, how can they learn? Without relaxation, no real learning is possible. This is the first lesson which clearly needs to be understood. It's very important that parents should understand this before they ask their children to do something. Amma suggests that they practice it in their own lives. For, unless they, themselves, experience the importance of relaxation, they won't know how important it is for their children. Spiritual practices such as meditation, repetition of a mantra, and singing bhajans, are different methods which are meant to relax the mind so that you can always be open like a freshly blossomed flower.

"Parents do not know the great harm they are doing their children by their constant whipping: 'Study, study, study!' When they arrange private tuition on every subject during holidays and weekends, the poor boys and girls have to literally rush from one teacher to another, exhausting all their energy and feeling very stressful. By the time the youngster gets back home in the evening, he is pale and exhausted; he cannot even eat his food with composure. The result is that the child cannot think about anything but his studies. He reads and reads, repeats endlessly and memorizes everything, as if he were feeding information into a computer. The child keeps on feeding and feeding, overloading and stuffing himself with more facts than he can possibly absorb.

"He or she may get record high marks and pass with distinction, but by the time the youngster finishes his education, he will be almost like a machine. He will no longer be able to experience the vibrancy, or the beauty and love of life, and he will lack any real wisdom. There will be no playfulness or laughter in his life. He is closed. As an adult he cannot even smile at his wife or be playful with his own children. He may be well-known and eminent in his field, but he will not be a successful human being. The luster of life will be absent in such a person. At home he will always be tight and serious. To always be extremely serious, whether it seems called for or not, is like a disease.

"When such people grow old, their faculties also wear out, because of the unintelligent methods by which they have gathered their knowledge. They have gathered information through their intense studies, during which they were never at ease, never relaxed. In this process they have used their inner faculties unwisely. They never allowed their mind to rest. It consequently got overused and overheated. They kept on feeding it non-stop; they never turned it off and let it be still for a time, so that it could relax and cool down. They never took care of their equipment, and now they are burned out."

As Mother's vibrant words carried the fragrance of Her divine presence into the hearts of the listeners, She began singing *Devi Jaganmata.* . .

> *Hail to the Goddess, the Mother of the world,*
> *The Goddess of Supreme Energy!*

O Eternal Virgin
Doing penance on the shore
Of the blue sea at Kanyakumari,
Come and give me a boon!

O Mother, whose true nature is Light
And whose beautiful form
Is made of wisdom, truth, energy and bliss!

Aum
Hail to the Mother of the Universe!

THE ART OF RELAXATION

The conversation continued.

Question: "Amma, You were talking about relaxation. Could You kindly elaborate a little more on this point?"

Mother: "Only through relaxed study can knowledge be retained. A study undertaken with stress and strain, without any relaxed, restful moments for the body, mind, or intellect, cannot be successful. In fact, it is relaxation that provides the clarity of vision and the energy necessary to learn and retain any real knowledge. The knowledge gathered in this way remains fresh forever, irrespective of your age. Whatever learning one does mechanically, under stressful and strenuous circumstances without any relaxation, will not help in the overall development of a person. Only someone who has gathered knowledge with a peaceful mind can really put that knowledge into practice and become a master in his field. Others will simply carry around the weight of their knowledge in their heads. They are carrying around a load of information, which they think is an embellishment to their personality, when, in fact, it has the opposite effect, for it disfigures their personality to a certain extent.

"There are hundreds of thousands of people all over the world who study the different sciences and other subjects. You can see Ph.D. holders springing up like mushrooms everywhere. There are also millions of engineers and medical doctors around the globe. But how many of them really benefit the world with their knowledge and their studies? How many among them become truly great in their fields? Only a few. Countless people also learn music and painting, but how many become soul-capturing artists or musicians? Only a handful. There are people who may have studied in the same college and with the same teacher; their circumstances may have been identical. Why, then, is it that only a few become true, renowned masters?

"It is because only a few of them have ever learned the art of relaxation. Only a few were at ease during their studies. The rest were just stuffed with information. They wanted to score high marks, get a decent job with a good salary, a nice house, a wife and children—and that was the end of it, the end of their studies. They put a full stop right there and began to worry about other things. Such people cannot stop worrying and are never at ease. They will always be under a lot of pressure and feel stressful, because they have never learned the art of relaxation.

"But a person who knows how to relax continues to learn new things. Throughout his life, his thirst for knowledge will remain ever fresh. He feels no tension; he is relaxed, and he therefore keeps on gathering knowledge, which he actually puts into practice. He not only studies about space, he invents new methods, new techniques and equipment with which to explore the subject. He not only learns about the under-sea world, he dives deep into the water to discover what is there. His curiosity is inexhaustible. Even though he has an unquenchable thirst to learn and to know, he is always relaxed, and this relaxed mood gives him the strength and vitality to absorb more knowledge and to put it into practice through his experiments. Such people can dive deep into their own Self, the Source of all knowledge, if they have the faith and determination. This will eventually help them to realize their true existence in the Self.

"There are poets, painters, musicians, and scientists who

spend a lot of time in solitude, contemplating and relaxing. They withdraw from the noisy world and go into seclusion. While sitting there in a fully relaxed mood, they withdraw from the mind and its thoughts. They will sometimes slip into a deep, trancelike state; and as they come out of that state they are able to create a great masterpiece. There have been many such incidents—but how does it happen? It is the outcome of the deep silence they feel within during such experiences. When the mind is devoid of thoughts, when there are no disturbances, no agitation whatsoever, an awakening takes place and the dormant talents, the infinite capacities of the mind, are manifested. Revelations occur as you tap into the unknown realms of pure, divine knowledge. This is the greatness of inner relaxation.

"So children, if you want to learn your lessons well, relaxation is the best method. It will keep your intellect clear, your memory power will increase tremendously, and you will not exhaust your energy by repeating a lesson a hundred times in order to memorize it. When you are deeply relaxed, you need only read the lesson once and you will know it forever.

"Have you ever seen the old grandparents chanting the entire text of a scripture, or a long Sanskrit hymn, without glancing at a text even once? They must have learned it when they were young. They were either taught by their parents or they must have listened to it being recited. They chant it so clearly and precisely without making any mistakes. Even when they are in their nineties, they chant it perfectly. What memories they have!

"A few years ago when Amma visited the house of some devotees, She met the grandmother of that family. She was ninety years old, gaunt like a skeleton and completely bed ridden. Her life was ebbing away but she could still speak. As Amma sat down next to her on the bed, the old woman's daughter said, 'Mother, open your eyes. Look who is sitting next to you! It's Amma!' The old lady slowly opened her eyes. With a beaming smile she looked up at Amma. As the old woman lay gazing at Amma's face her daughter said, 'Mother, chant the *Narayaneeyam* for Amma.' Before the daughter had finished the sentence the old lady began to chant the Sanskrit *slokas* fluently, with absolute clarity. She continued to chant for a long time without showing any sign of tiredness until, finally, her daughter had to tell her to stop.

"Children, look at Acchamma.[6] She is nearly eighty, but she still gets up at four in the morning, takes a bath in cold water, repeats her regular chants; and every day, without fail, she makes a garland for Amma to wear during Devi Bhava.

"In the olden days people were much more relaxed than

---

[6] Mother's paternal grandmother

they are now. There was no hurry. They always managed to find some free time to read the scriptures, chant the verses from the epics, and to sing the glories of the Lord in a peaceful and relaxed atmosphere.

"Every morning and evening, the whole family gathered in the family shrine room to pray together and sing the names of the Supreme Lord. Those moments of relaxation, which they found in the midst of their active day to day lives, helped them perform their work in the world in a well balanced frame of mind.

"Look at the above example of the old woman reciting the Sanskrit *slokas* from the *Narayaneeyam*, even on her death bed. How could she do this? Because it hadn't been fed into her as if she were a computer. She absorbed it like an intelligent human being with a relaxed, tension-free mind, and she loved it. Whatever you study, if you do so in a relaxed mood, it will remain fresh with you until the day you die; whereas, whatever you learn in a tense and stressful mood will soon be forgotten. In reality, you cannot learn anything without relaxation—it doesn't enter into you. It will remain only at the surface, and whatever is at the surface of the mind is bound to be forgotten. It is like the ephemeral waves of the sea that come and go. Whatever knowledge is gathered by a mind that isn't relaxed, that knowledge will not take root but will be subject to change and distortions. The mind can subsequently only provide you with unclear pictures.

"Children, learn to be relaxed in all circumstances. Whatever you do and wherever you are, relax and you will see how powerful it is. The art of relaxation brings out the power that exists within you; through relaxation you can experience your infinite capacities. It is the art of making your mind still, and of focusing all your energy on the work you are doing, whatever it may be. Thus you will be able to bring out all your potential. Once you learn this art, every-thing happens spontaneously and effortlessly. For example, you want to memorize a speech or a poem; so you sit down and relax, dropping everything else from your mind, and you go through the subject just once—not a hundred times while forgoing food and sleep—and you get it, once and for all. It stays with you forever. Within the human mind infinite capacities lie hidden. It can accommodate the entire uni-verse and all the knowledge in it. But we haven't learned the art of tapping into that infinite power of the mind."

Mother stopped talking while one of the women devo-tees was inspired to sing a few verses from the *Uddhava Gita*.[7] She sang it melodiously in the classical way.

---

[7] A chapter from the Srimad Bhagavatam. It is a conversation between Lord Krishna and His great devotee, Uddhava.

Lord, to Thy Lotus Feet, which those seeking liberation from the strong meshes of work fervently meditate upon within the heart, we bow with our buddhi, organs, vital powers, manas, and speech.

O Thou Invincible One, through Thy maya consisting of the three gunas, and resting in them, Thou dost create, maintain, and destroy in Thyself this unthinkable universe; but these activities do not touch Thee, for Thou art unimpeachable, being immersed in the unobstructed bliss of the Self.

O Adorable One! O Supreme! Mental worship, scriptural study, charity, austerities, and work do not confer such purity on men of unsatisfied desires as the men of balanced minds obtain through a heightened true regard for Thy glories, developed by means of hearing (of them).

When she finished the last verse, Mother looked at her affectionately and said, "Daughter, you chanted beautifully." The woman was pleased and happy. She said, "It is Your Grace, Amma."

The stream of Mother's nectarous words continued to flow. "Children, have you heard this story? A long time ago there was an emperor who conquered India. The Emperor also had another intention: he wanted to take all the four Vedas in their pure, original form back to his country. The Emperor sent his messengers to several parts of India to find out where he could get a genuine copy of the Vedas. Eventually he received the information that one such copy was preserved by a Brahmin family in northern India. He immediately set off to that part of the country with a whole battalion of soldiers.

"The Brahmin, who was the head of the family, was a poor man who lived with his wife and four sons in a small hut on the banks of the river Ganges. The Emperor commanded his forces to surround the hut, whereupon he entered the dwelling and ordered the Brahmin to surrender the Vedas to him. The Brahmin was very calm. He replied, 'Your Highness, surely there is no need to make such a fuss. I will happily hand them over to you! But give me one day—just one day. I have a special ceremony to perform before I can give them to you.' When he saw the suspicious look on the Emperor's face the Brahmin continued, 'Do not worry, let your army remain here if you wish. Let them keep an eye on me. I'm not going to run away. Be kind enough to come back tomorrow morning, for I must do this ritual before I can hand the Vedas over to you.'"

"The Emperor left, having given his troops the necessary instructions. But what did he see when he returned the
next morning and entered the hut! He saw the Brahmin
offering the last page of the fourth Veda into a sacrificial
fire, as he loudly chanted the mantras of that page. His four
sons were seated on either side of the fire, with the Brahmin
at its head. The Emperor was furious. He shouted at the
Brahmin, 'You have betrayed me! I will have you beheaded
for this!' The Brahmin remained very calm and replied, 'Your
Highness, there is no need to be angry. Please look at my
four sons. They have been sitting by my side the whole night,
listening as I chanted all the Vedas, one by one. As you saw,
I have just finished the fourth and last Veda. Do not think
that I have cheated you by destroying the Vedas, or that I
have broken my promise. Believe me or not, my sons have
memorized all the four Vedas, word for word. They have
listened to me. They can repeat the entire scripture without
missing a single word. Take my sons with you to your country. They are capable of imparting the knowledge in all its
original purity.'

"The Emperor couldn't believe it. He said, 'This is unthinkable! I don't trust you.' The Brahmin then asked his
sons to chant the Vedas, and to the astonishment of the
Emperor, they chanted all four of them beautifully, without

making a single mistake. Remember, they had studied it all in a single night. They simply listened intently and with great love to their father as he chanted, and it went straight to their hearts. Thus they could memorize everything so spontaneously.

"But see how it is today. The students learn something by repeating it countless times; and yet, they may still forget it when they later have to stand up and recite it in front of everyone in the classroom. The problem here is fear.

"Magicians, mathematicians, scientist, musicians, painters and others develop only an infinitesimal portion of the power that is inherent within them. Only a true master, who is established in the Atman, has tapped into that infinite power source which exists within us all."

Mother stopped talking and in a sudden change of mood, Her face took on the expression of an innocent child. Mother turned around and in a begging tone asked one of the brahmacharinis, who was classically trained, to sing the song, *Nilambuja Nayane.*

> *O Mother, with blue lotus eyes*
> *Don't You hear the cries*
> *Of this sorrowing heart?*
> *Is it due to the deeds of some past life*

That I am wandering alone?
I have passed through the ages
Before being born again in this life.

Please draw me close to You
With a motherly hug;
Let me curl up in Your lap
Like a child;
O Mother, I may not deserve You
But will You forsake this child for that reason?
Come and hold me close to You
Envelope me in Your merciful glance.

THE TECHNIQUE

After a short silence another question was put forth.

"How does the technique of relaxation work?"

Mother: "Children, when you relax you forget everything. A space is created and your mind becomes empty. Suppose you are sitting in a park with your beloved by your side. Many different things are happening in the park. People are gossiping or talking about the recent political changes, children are playing, youngsters are shouting, screaming and merry-making; but you and your lover, sitting in a corner gazing into each other's eyes, are unaware of what is happening around you. When all thoughts are put aside and forgotten, you are filled with the sweet fragrance of love, and the heart is allowed to blossom. At that moment, everything stops—even you and your beloved cease to exist. There is only love. At that moment, yesterday and tomorrow can no longer interfere. When the past and the future dissolve, love will arise, and only out of that love can real relaxation be experienced.

"In the same way, when you are relaxed you forget everything else; and in that forgetful mood, if you focus all your energy on something of your choice, the whole subject just enters into you. At that moment your whole being is wide open—every atom, every cell of your body is so receptive that you can just swallow the whole subject and digest it.

"This is the method that the rishis used in the education of their disciples. They made their disciples forget everything and relax. In that atmosphere of love and openness all their previous conditioning was forgotten.

"The disciples who studied at the gurukulas belonged to all classes of society. From the royal prince to the son of the poorest man, they all studied in the same hermitage, under the same master. Normally, in such a situation, there would be plenty of opportunities for all kinds of divisions and conflicts to occur. Can you imagine how all those children, coming from entirely different backgrounds, and with different mental dispositions, could stay in the same hermitage, where the conditions and facilities were usually very Spartan? They led a hard life. Most hermitages in those days were situated in the forests, far away from any town or village. The Master never treated the disciples differently; he never provided a prince with a separate, beautifully furnished bedroom, along with a bunch of servants to take care of his needs, nor did he put the son of a poor man in a musty, dusty, matchbox-sized hut. There was no such discrimination with food, accommodation or clothing. They ate the same food, slept on the same floor, and they all wore simple clothes. Whether it was a prince, the child of a minister or a nobleman, or the son of a poor man, they all had to adjust to the same simple way of living, and they worked hard. There was absolutely no division or partiality. On the other hand, there was much sharing, deep love, and a feeling of oneness among them.

"It was the quality of the Master that was the source of all the beauty and charm in their lives. It was his presence that helped the disciples forget all divisions and live in oneness, and to drink in the knowledge imparted by the Master.

"So, My children, remember: only through love and relaxation is it possible to grow. But unfortunately, our concept about what growth really is has changed. We believe that growth is something external: become rich, buy as many cars, houses, as much property and as many stocks as you can; then people will say, 'He has grown tremendously!' This is the sort of comment we would make about such a person. We think he has developed, but is it real growth? As long as one is divided within, one cannot grow. The majority of human beings are divided, both within and without. How can any real development take place in a person, or in society, as long as there is no love or sense of unity?

"Real growth takes place in the unity that is born out of love. The milk that flows out of the mother's breast nourishes the baby and provides its body with strength and vitality, allowing all the organs to grow healthily and in proportion. But it is not just milk that flows out of the mother's breast— it is the warmth, the love and affection of the mother in the form of milk. In a similar way, love is the 'breast milk' that helps society to grow as a whole. Love provides the necessary strength and vitality which enables society to grow without division."

CHAPTER SEVEN

THE MOTHER OF THE UNIVERSE

*I*t was five o'clock in the afternoon. Mother was standing in front of the cow shed with a group of brahmacharis, brahmacharinis and visiting householder devo-tees. The cows were tied up outside and were being led into the cow shed by a brahmachari. As the brahmachari was about to untie the last cow, Mother said to him, "Son, wait a minute." Mother smiled and approached the cow. She suddenly got down on Her hands and knees like a small child and began drinking milk directly from the udders of the cow. The cow stood very still with a look of tremendous bliss on her face. As Mother drank from each udder, the udders were filled with more and more milk. Mother looked so utterly sweet and innocent with the milk trickling down Her cheeks.

Those who watched this unique scene were deeply moved, because it reminded them of the stories of Sri Krishna's childhood. The cow must have accumulated a great deal of merit to be given the opportunity to feed the Universal Mother directly from its udders.

Finally, Mother stood up. She wiped Her face with a towel

and kissed the cow affectionately. She said, "Children, this cow has been waiting for Mother to drink from her for a long time. Her desire for this was very strong."

One of the devotees said with great feeling, "Amma, You are truly the Mother of the Universe. You can understand the thoughts and feelings of all of Creation and act accordingly.

Mother walked towards the back of the cow shed. The brahmachari untied the cow and as the cow was being led into the cow shed, she turned her head towards Mother and kept gazing at Her.

Mother said, "Children, there was a time when everybody, even Amma's parents, were against Her because of Her unusual ways, and they abandoned Her. When that happened, it was the birds and the animals who took care of Amma's needs. A dog used to bring food packets for Amma from somewhere. Sometimes Amma would sit in deep samadhi for several days at a stretch. When She came out of that state, a cow would come and stand in front of Her in such a position that Amma could drink as much as She wanted directly from its udders. There was an eagle who was in the habit of bringing fish for Amma, which She ate raw. Children, when you are one with Creation, when your heart is filled with nothing but love, all of Nature will be your friend and will serve you. It is your selfishness and narrow-mindedness that is keeping the creatures away."

Mother was now standing behind the cow shed. When She noticed that the tank that collected the cow urine was full to overflowing, She said, "Children, Amma is surprised to see that none of you have taken the initiative to empty this tank." Mother then summoned the brahmachari who was in charge of the cows and asked, "Didn't you see this? Isn't it your duty to make sure that the cow shed and its surroundings are kept clean? Children, it doesn't matter what you do. The important thing is how you do it. If you don't perform your actions with love and dedication, how can you progress spiritually? Amma doesn't want to say much. You children should learn to do things willingly and spontaneously without having to be asked." Having said this, Mother Herself began emptying the tank with a bucket. When they saw this, the whole group came forward. At first they were afraid to approach Mother in case She was angry and wouldn't let them help. But Mother didn't say anything. Taking this as a sign, they fetched more buckets and began to help, and within a few minutes the tank was clean. By the time the work was done, Mother's dress was covered with dirt. But Mother didn't care. She grabbed a broom that was lying in a corner and began sweeping the whole area around the cow shed. Though everyone begged Mother to let them do it, She continued to sweep until the place looked clean.

It was time for the evening bhajans. Mother went to Her room and returned a few minutes later to let everyone drink in the bliss of Her soulful song.

FEAR BLOCKS SPONTANEITY

When the bhajans were over Mother again graciously answered some questions. The devotees were delighted at the opportunity to tap into the knowledge of this infinite source of wisdom.

Question: "Amma, the other day, you said that one cannot be relaxed if one is gripped by fear, and thus one fails to express oneself spontaneously. What causes this fear?"

Mother: "It is the thought of what others may think of us that causes this fear. It is the fear of judgment. The problem lies in the feeling of otherness. As long as this fear remains, your heart will be closed, and a closed heart cannot express itself.

"Take the example of the student who is asked to recite a poem in front of the class. He learns the poem by repeating it in the solitude of his home; but when the student later tries to recite the poem in front of the others he is overcome by fear—the fear of judgment. He is overwhelmed by the thought of what his friends and the teacher will think of him if he makes a mistake, and so he suddenly forgets all that he has learned.

"When the student is alone behind the closed doors of his room, he is relaxed and unafraid. In the midst of others, however, he cannot relax. The thought that they are watching him and that they may judge and criticize, creates a block within him and he loses his ability to express himself. A feeling of otherness creates this fear and blocks the flow of inspiration and expression. The feeling of otherness should disappear if we are to express ourselves fully. We should learn to always feel as relaxed as we do in the solitude of our own room.

"A beautiful song will only come from a singer who forgets both the audience and himself. A heart-capturing painting will emerge only when the artist forgets himself and everything else, even the world. All sense of otherness must disappear if your talents are to be expressed in all their fullness and beauty. The feeling of otherness obstructs the flow of your heart.

"Amma knows a boy who is a very talented singer. He has a wonderful voice, but whenever he tries to sing in front of others, he utterly fails to express his gift; he trembles, breaks out in a sweat and sings off key. Poor boy! In his fear of judgment, he is overwhelmed by thoughts such as, 'How am I going to sing in front of all these people? Will my singing please them? Will I be able to sing properly? If I don't, what will they think of me?' It then becomes impossible for him to sing in front of an audience.

"Look at a Mahatma. Whenever he wants, he can express his whole being with all its charm and beauty. He is not conditioned by anything. The feeling of otherness is absent in him, and he is fearless. He can move and mingle freely with anyone at any time, no matter where he is. How is this possible? It is possible because he beholds everyone as his own Self. For him, there is only the Self."

It sounded as if Mother was speaking about Herself. A person who observes Mother will soon notice how freely Mother mingles with people and spontaneously adjusts to different situations without the least feeling of unfamiliarity. No one is a stranger to Her, nor do people perceive Her as a stranger in any way. This helps people to open up and share all their feelings with Mother. They feel that Mother is very close to them, that She is their very own. And this is true—no one can be closer to us than Mother—for She is our own innermost Self. The feeling of otherness is totally absent in Her. Being beyond all fears, Mother can express Her whole being in any situation.

ALONENESS AND LONELINESS

Question: "What is the difference between being lonely and inner solitude?"

Mother: "Aloneness (inner solitude) helps you to relax. Aloneness has nothing to do with loneliness. You can feel lonely when you are overwhelmed by thoughts and emotions. Imagine that you are living a happy family life, your workplace is close to your home, you love to spend time with your family, and then your office suddenly sends you abroad for two years. You are asked to go immediately and you can't take your family with you. So you leave your home to settle down in a new place. When you get there you feel intensely sad. You seem to lose all your strength and enthusiasm. You cannot stop thinking about your wife and children. The separation from your family makes you lonely, and the more you miss your family the more vulnerable you feel. When you are lonely you become emotionally upset, and when you are upset you become vulnerable. You become the slave of your mind. In that state you are an easy victim of any situation, and as a result you lose your peace of mind. A lonely person is agitated and cannot feel peaceful or happy. This is what loneliness does to you.

"Aloneness, on the other hand, is something that happens deep within; it makes you feel contented and at peace in any situation. Whether you are physically alone, or in the midst of a big crowd of strange people in a foreign country with a different culture and language, you will be immensely happy and you will be spontaneous in the way you express yourself. A person who has developed this inner aloneness cannot be overpowered by emotions. He will never feel sad or empty. Nothing can upset the spontaneous flow of his heart when he is in this state.

"Whereas you feel lonely when you are enslaved by the mind, aloneness is a state you enter when you become the master of your mind, when you go beyond the mind. Loneliness is external, it is of the mind and body. Aloneness is internal, it belongs to the Atman. Loneliness is the outcome of attachment. Aloneness is the outcome of detachment. Loneliness plunges you into a state of darkness and sorrow. Aloneness brings light and love into your life.

"Aloneness is not the same as seclusion. When we are in a beautiful picturesque place, away from the crowd, we are in seclusion. But in that sort of solitude, one can still be agitated, if aloneness, or *inner* solitude, has not been attained.

"You feel lonely when you are tense and agitated. Aloneness, on the other hand, is experienced when you are relaxed and free of all tension. Loneliness closes your heart and blocks off every possibility of self-expression. Aloneness helps you to open up fully and to express yourself naturally and spontaneously. Loneliness is the sign of a person who is bound by the world and its objects, and by desires. Aloneness is the sign of a soul who is free from all desires and the objects and pleasures of the world."

Question: "How can we attain this state of aloneness? How can we let go of all our fears and our feelings of otherness?"

Mother: "This is possible only through meditation. In order to feel completely relaxed and to finally reach the state of perfect aloneness, the interference of the past and the future should stop. Only this moment exists and should be experienced. Meditation is the technique of knowing how to be in the present moment.

"By concentrating on, for example, a form, sound, or light, we learn to constantly be in that state of inner aloneness, and to be joyful in any situation. To be content in one's own Self, by the Self, and for the Self, is what is known as inner aloneness. All spiritual practices are done in order to experience this aloneness or one-pointedness of mind. In reality, we don't have to depend on anything external for our happiness. We should become independent—depending only on our own Self, the very Source of all joy. A true Master's presence is the best place for this aloneness to be experienced.

"Don't confuse this state of aloneness with being physically alone in a quiet place. Unless you have silenced your
mind, you will not find that inner aloneness even if you sit
in a quiet spot, in a beautiful cave in the Himalayas, or in a
pleasant, secluded forest. If the mind is noisy you won't
experience real aloneness, but will continue to remain in the
grip of the mind and its negativity.

"Once, three seekers went to the mountains to do serious
sadhana. Before starting they decided to take a vow of silence for three years. All three of them then began doing
severe austerities. One day a horse happened to pass by. Almost
a year went by when one fine morning one of them said,
'That was a beautiful white horse.' That was all he said. There
was no more speaking after that. Thus another year went by,
when one day the second man suddenly remarked. "No, that
wasn't a white horse. It was a black horse.' That was it. Again
silence prevailed for a whole year. When finally the three
years had come to an end, the third person opened his mouth
and said, "Enough is enough! I am leaving this place right
now! You two have no discipline and you are disturbing others
with your talk as well.'"

Everyone laughed at Mother's story.

"Children, that inner aloneness can be experienced only
when the mind is still and silent. From that stillness the

beautiful flower of peace and bliss will emerge. Once that aloneness is experienced, you can be anywhere on this planet or in any other world, even in the netherworld, but you will always be immersed in bliss and peace. It doesn't matter if you are physically alone or in the noisiest place in the world—you are always joyful and contented.

"A Satguru will create situations through which this aloneness can be found within you. The Master doesn't teach anything, but in his presence helpful situations spontaneously arise. This can happen because the Master is the embodiment of 'That.' He is the creator of each situation that will allow you to grow spiritually. The Master helps you to close the doors and windows of your senses. Your senses are the doors and windows through which you stray away from your inner Self. You cannot see the Self through the doors and windows of the senses. In reality, you don't need them to see your Self.

"Suppose you are living in the most wonderful, picturesque surroundings. You are in your house and you suddenly wish to take a look at the beautiful landscape outside. You open the door and walk out into that landscape, or you may stay inside and look out through the window. But if you want to take a look at yourself, there is no need to go outside. You can close the door and turn away from it, because you know that you are not to be found somewhere out there; you are here within. You need the outlets of the senses to perceive the external world, but through those senses you cannot experience the inner Self; for that Self is not to be found somewhere out there in the world. The Self cannot be seen through the eyes or experienced through any of the senses, which are all focused outwardly, in the opposite direction of your Self. If you wish to see the Self, you have to become blind; you have to close the doors and stop directing your focus outwardly, because the Self is within. Once you realize your true, indwelling Self, you can go out through the doors of your senses as much as you wish, for then you no longer see a world of diversity—everything is transformed into one totality. But for this to happen you have to become blind to this world of plurality. When you become blind to the outer world, even when your eyes are open, that is when you de-velop the divine, inner eye, a new vision—the third eye of infinite knowledge and wisdom. That is what you see in a Mahatma's eyes.

"Meditation is the technique that allows you to shut the doors and windows of the senses, so that your can look within and see your Self. Real meditation can only be experienced in the presence of a Satguru. A true Master is constantly in meditation, even though you may see him being physically active. His presence is the most conducive place for your Self-unfolding to take place. In his presence you can attain that inner aloneness and thereby get rid of all your fears and feelings of otherness."

Mother paused, and in the silence of the night She began to sing, *Nilameghangale . . .*

> *O blue clouds!*
> *How did you get that azure tone today,*
> *The charming dark-blue complexion*
> *Of the Child of Nanda in Vrindavan?*
>
> *Did you meet the Child, Kannan Krishna?*
> *Did you talk to each other*
> *And exchange a smile?*
> *Did the glance of His eyes*
> *Blue as the lotus*
> *Caress you from head to toe?*
>
> *Did Kannan tell you*
> *When He will appear before me?*
> *Did He say that He would welcome me also?*
> *Did He send a few consoling words*
> *through you*
> *For the peace of my mind?*

SELF-EFFORT IN THE SATGURU'S PRESENCE

As they heard the sound of Mother singing, more residents came out of their huts and gathered around Her. When the song came to an end, Mother sat quietly looking up at the beautiful sky that was lit by the moon and numerous twinkling stars. After a few minutes, another question was asked.

"Amma, it sounds as if everything simply happens in the presence of a true Master, without any self-effort on our part. But isn't self-effort necessary for the inner eye to open?"

Mother: "Children, even self-effort happens spontaneously in the presence of a Master, provided you have the right attitude, faith, and understanding. The intensity of the situations created by the Master is such that self-effort happens without our knowledge. Just as a bud opens up into a beautiful, fragrant flower, you will also experience yourself opening up naturally and spontaneously in the presence of a Satguru.

"Of course, there is such a thing as self-effort; but for that effort to bear the right fruit we must first know what is to be done and how. Only a perfect Master can bestow this knowledge upon us. Through our constant companionship with the Master, it becomes known to us, and from there on it is easy. You think that something has to be done to attain liberation; but the point of the Guru-sishya relationship is to let the disciple know that there is nothing to be done, because *Moksha* (Liberation) is not something that comes to you or enters into you from outside; on the contrary, it is something that is intrinsically part of you, something that you already are.

"The mind, or the past, is not the problem; the problem lies in your identification with the mind, with your past. The unintelligent attachment, the feeling of 'I and mine,' is the problem. Once you learn the art of withdrawing your attachment and being a witness, then something changes in the way you see everything.

"Amma has heard a story that She will use as an example. A factory is on fire. The owner of the factory is in a terrible state, sobbing and screaming like one gone mad. 'Everything is being destroyed!' he cries. 'All my wealth, everything that I have earned through hard work is gone. I'm ruined!' Then suddenly, a friend comes up to him and says, 'Why are you crying so desperately? Don't you know that your son sold the factory yesterday? It is no longer yours!' The factory is still burning, the situation hasn't changed, but the man immediately stops crying. The burning within him has stopped. He wipes his tears and smiles relieved. Just then, his son comes and tells him, 'Dad, why are you just standing there? Don't you see that the factory is in flames? Why don't you do something!' The father says, 'What is there to do? You have sold the factory.' But the son tells him, 'No, father, we almost sold the factory yesterday but something went wrong; the sale didn't go through.' As soon as he learns the news, the father is again thrown into a state of despair, and his sobbing is resumed.

"The burning building is not the cause of his suffering. His attachment to the building is the real reason for his suffering. The thought that the factory is his, and then later that it is no longer his, creates entirely different moods in him. His initial terror and despair changes into happiness and relief, and then again back to despair. The outer situation hasn't changed as the factory continues to burn—the changes happen within him. When he hears that the factory has been sold, he withdraws his attachment and just witnesses the building being burned. But as soon as he receives the news that the building hasn't been sold after all, an attachment is created which plunges him back into sorrow. If you can renounce your feelings of attachment, then you will always be calm. Stop identifying with the world created by your mind, and a new world will open up before you. You may still own a big house, a beautiful car and other comforts, but you don't really possess anything. By not letting any insentient objects affect your life, you become their master.

"Don't think that all your memories of the past will disappear when you attain the state of Perfection. No, the memories are still there, but you will never again identify with them. Once your identification with the past is withdrawn, the past becomes no more than a storage place for your memories. Think of the past as a storage place and not as the place where you live. If you need to use something from the past, you go to there and fetch it, and as soon as you have found what you need, you leave the place. You do not live there. This is what needs to be understood. Don't spend your life in the storage place of your past, for that is not your home. Come away from there and live in the light, the love, and the freedom where you belong. This is the message of a true Master. You will learn it by just being in his presence. Nowhere else in the world can this be learned."

CHAPTER EIGHT

LIKE THE SHINING SUN
AND THE EVER-BLOWING WIND

The concrete work of the new prayer hall had started early today. Almost all the Ashram residents were working hard, carrying the concrete in big metal pans which they passed on to each other. Soon after they had begun, Mother arrived at the site and was about to participate in the work. Br. Balu[8] pleaded with Her and said, "Amma, this is concrete work. Please don't do this! Why do You worry when there are so many people here to do the work? Amma, the material will burn your skin if it happens to spill on You."

Mother replied "It will burn your skin as well, not only Amma's."

But Balu persisted, "Amma, please don't do this! We will do the work."

Mother smiled at him and said, "Son, Amma is happy to do any kind of work. From a very young age, Amma had to work hard. Her body never knew what rest was. Don't worry."

Several others also tried to dissuade Mother from join-

---

[8] Swami Amritaswarupananda.

ing in the work. But their pleas fell on deaf ears. With a radiant smile, Mother tied a cloth around Her head and began working beside Her children. She lifted a metal pan filled with concrete onto Her head, and carried it away.

Everyone was engrossed in work when one concrete-filled container suddenly slipped and fell from a brahmachari's hands heavily onto the ground. He managed to step back the moment before it fell, so that he didn't hurt his feet. But the cement splashed and made a few marks on Mother's face. The brahmachari said, "Amma, please forgive me for my lack of shraddha." Mother smiled at him and said, "No problem! This is just part of the play." Mother wiped Her face with a towel handed to Her by one of the brahmacharis and continued to work. As they worked Mother chanted, "Om Namah Shivaya," and everyone responded in a chorus. This was followed by another song, *Adiyil Parameswariye. . .*

> *O Primal, Supreme Goddess*
> *O Mother of all the worlds*
> *I have no goal in this world*
> *Except Mother.*
>
> *O Mother, with beautiful eyes*
> *Like the petals of a blue lotus,*
> *You are the Sustainer of the three worlds.*

O Dweller in the lotus flower, Maya
O Beautiful One
The Source of everything
Rid me of all sorrows.

O Gracious One
Destroyer of greed
Who leads us through
the land of transmigration
Protect me.
O Mother, Giver of devotion and liberation
O Katyayani, far-famed One
I bow to You.

O Goddess of the earth
Who is wisdom and knowledge
The only delight and the only nourishment
You are all of Creation.
O Fulfiller of all desires
Please rid me of my pride
Dwell within my mind and remove my desires.

Mother was standing in the blazing sun. A devotee tried to hold an umbrella over Her head, but Mother lovingly refused and moved away saying, "No, no! How can Amma use an umbrella when all Her children are working in the sun?"

It was getting hotter. Beads of sweat glittered on Mother's beautiful face. Mother had been working continuously for the last two hours, but Her smile never faded for a moment. She wiped Her face with a towel and said, "Children, as you work, try to feel God's presence everywhere. Just imagine that all those who are working with you are sparks of Divinity. God is carrying sand; God is passing the concrete to God; the masonry, the people who are mixing the cement, the metal pans—everything is pervaded with God-consciousness. Try to do the work with this feeling. Then your time will not be wasted."

Mother continued to work. At one point She put the metal pan down. Now there was only the cloth wrapped like a turban around Her head. She looked so cute and attractive, that some of the residents paused in their work just to look at Mother, and their faces lit up with a smile.

Just then, a group of young men, who were long time devotees of Mother, came to see Her. They had brought a few new people with them. Mother removed the turban and walked with them towards the front of the meditation hall. Br. Balu and two other brahmacharis joined the group, knowing that Mother was bound to talk about spiritual subjects with the young men, who were inquisitive and sincere.

After offering their prostrations to Mother, one of the young men said, "Amma, it looks as if You have been working for a long time. You must be tired."

"Son," Mother replied, "You will feel tired only if there is no love in your actions. You cannot be overcome by tiredness and boredom if your actions are done with love."

After some light conversation, one of the newcomers asked Mother a question.

WHETHER OR NOT YOU BELIEVE
YOUR DIVINITY REMAINS UNCHANGED

Question: "Amma, spirituality recommends that we eliminate our ego. But what is the use of dropping the ego? I believe that the ego is useful—it's not a useless thing. It's only because of the ego that this beautiful world exists. If this world is going to disappear when the ego is destroyed, I would rather cling to my ego. If I have a choice, I'll keep my ego. I won't let it go."

Mother: "Son, you cannot force anyone to drop his ego. Nobody likes to let go of the ego—it is so precious to everyone. However, once you have attained the state of egolessness, the world won't disappear, as you may think it will. The world will continue, but a change takes place within you. Something is uncovered. You start seeing everything with the wonder and innocence of a child.

"When you realize the Self, the entire universe attains realization, as it were; because, in that state, you realize the all-pervasive nature of the Atman. You behold and experience the Atman everywhere. As the realization that everything is pervaded with Divine Consciousness dawns within you, you also see that every human being, everything in creation, is already Divine. The only difference is that you know that you and they are one with Divinity, but they do not. It is only a question of uncovering the truth.

"Son, whether you drop your ego or not, Divinity is your true nature. Nothing can change that. If you insist on saying that 'I am the ego, body, mind, and intellect,' it won't make any difference. Your true nature isn't in the least affected by your lack of understanding. It is like saying that the earth is flat and not round. If you keep preaching that the earth is flat, believing it to be true, is it going to change the shape of the earth in any way? No, of course not. Similarly, you are free to believe that you are the ego and that the ego is real, but you will nevertheless continue to remain what you are: the Self (Atman). Your divine nature will not change or be diminished, even if you don't believe in it.

"If someone believes that fire is cold and ice is hot, will it make the fire cold and the ice hot? No, that would be impossible. It is the same with you and your true nature.

"You may say that the round shape of the earth and the hot and cold temperatures of fire and ice are proven facts; whereas the Self, our true nature, is only a question of faith. Son, before it was proven that the earth is round, it was only a belief based on faith, wasn't it? There was a difference of opinion among scientists concerning the shape of the earth; people even thought that the earth was flat. Later, it was proven that the earth is round; but until then, the shape of the earth remained a mystery, a matter of faith. Before scientists are able to prove anything, they simply believe. They work on the basis of a certain hypothesis, and when it has been proven through their experiments, they declare it to be true. So everything is a question of faith until it is experienced directly or proven scientifically.

"Just as scientists have proven their different theories through the work they do in their laboratories, the saints and sages, having worked in their inner laboratories, have experienced the Self, the Ultimate Reality, directly. This is not the experience of one or two persons at a particular place in history; it is the experience of all those around the globe who have explored their inner Self. So you cannot deny its authenticity by saying that it is only a belief and not something that is based on fact.

ONLY A BUD CAN BLOOM

"Keep your ego if you wish and don't let go of it. Nobody is going to force you to drop it, because force won't work here. It is like opening the petals of a flower. The bud has to open up naturally without any external force. Only the natural process of blossoming will bring out all the beauty and fragrance of a flower. However, if you become impatient and forcibly try to pull the petals open, the flower will die. Force will only destroy the inner process of opening up.

"When a bud has been closed for a long time, it feels an intense longing to open up, to come out and to dance joyfully in the fresh breeze of open space. The bud stage is like a prison. Being imprisoned creates a longing for freedom; it creates an intense thirst to break the bondage and come out. You could say it is an inevitable law that to really know the joy of freedom one must first be bound and imprisoned. For only a bud can bloom. Before the flower blossoms, it has to go through the stage of being a closed bud. The urge to open up arises out of the bud stage.

"In a similar way, your heart in its closed stage is known as the ego. At some point before it opens up, the bud may think, 'I am a bud and I like it this way. This world is so beautiful! If I had a choice I'd rather stay right here. They say there's a much higher state known as being a flower, a state full of beauty and fragrance. They talk about the colorful petals and the exquisite perfume that I have. But I myself know nothing of this; I am quite comfortable and secure as I am. Actually, I am afraid to change. . . .'

"You can remain where you are and argue as much as you like, but it won't last for long. The bud will soon begin to feel uncomfortable—a bit restless, a feeling of suffocation—and these feelings will intensify. As the suffocating feeling increases, an unquenchable thirst to come out and free yourself will also develop; and this will slowly culminate in your full unfolding and blossoming.

"The bud stage of the heart is the ego. You are experiencing the same trepidation as the bud: 'This world is beautiful as it is. I am afraid it might all disappear. If I have a choice, I'd rather cling to my ego.' You can rationalize like that, it's all right; but no matter how much you argue, the fact remains that you are a potential flower. Every single bud is a potential flower; it may be a bud now, but that doesn't mean that the latent flower isn't there. It is an unchangeable fact that there is a flower waiting to unfold within each unopened bud. You may be skeptical and deny it, but none of your thoughts can change the truth. Your thoughts and your doubts belong to the mind. No, the Truth cannot be changed. The Truth remains the Truth—indisputable and unchangeable.

"In a way, it is good to remain for as long as possible as a bud, in the closed stage of the ego, because the longer you stay in that condition, the more you will long to break out of it. The longer you are in jail, the more intense will be your longing to enjoy the bliss of freedom. Likewise, the more time you spend inside the closed shell of your ego, the more momentum you will gain for the final breakthrough to happen. So, it's good. Don't be in a hurry; stay in the shell and continue to rationalize and argue for as long as you like. It's a good sign, for it means that you are getting closer.

"But remember: nobody is going to force you to open up; you cannot be forced to drop your ego. If your choice is to cling to your ego, that's fine. You prefer the dark world of the bud; you feel comfortable there. Your mind has become so accustomed to the darkness within the closed bud that in your ignorance you believe that the darkness contains all the light you need. You don't know that the faint light you perceive is only the few pitiful rays of light that manage to enter through the minute cracks of the bud. It is like the dim light you'd get in a dungeon.

"It is as if you have spent such a long time in a dungeon that you have forgotten what true light is. 'This dungeon is enough for me,' you say to yourself. 'There is no brighter light than this. I don't want anything else.' Even if someone were to tell you about the brilliant sunlight that is available outside the dungeon, you would say, 'No, it can't be true.' But the sun exists and its light is the truth. How could it cease to exist, just because you happen to deny it? The problem lies within yourself, and has nothing to do with the sun or its light. You have to come out and experience the light. But you feel secure inside your dungeon and are afraid to come out. You are concerned about what would happen if you were to leave. Your concern is quite understandable, because you don't know anything about what lies beyond the dungeon. In your situation, you have no other source of information, except the words of the person who says to you, 'Look, my friend, there is a wonderful, radiant world out there! It is full of sunlight, beautiful mountains and valleys, sparkling rivers, blossoming trees; there is a moon and countless twinkling stars to be seen. Come with me. I know everything about it because I live there. Come, my friend, I will help you to be free.' You just have to trust him and believe in his words. Surrender to him and take a few courageous steps, so that you may know what he is talking about. He says to you, 'My friend, you are not free at all; you are in jail, bound in chains. Follow me, and I will show you the path to freedom. Take my hand and I will lead you there.'

"Nothing will happen if you resist saying, 'No, it isn't true! This dungeon is the most beautiful world there is. I prefer to be here. This light is the only light, and, as far as I'm concerned, there is no such thing as the sun, the moon or the stars.'

"However, sooner or later the jail itself is bound to create an instinctive urge within you, a longing to experience the bliss of freedom. Every human being, consciously or unconsciously, has a desire to be free and to be at peace in all circumstances. A breakthrough is therefore bound to happen at some point.

"The self-created shell of the ego should break open so that the heart can express itself fully.

But the ego can only be broken through the pain of love. Just as the seedling emerges when the outer shell of the seed breaks open, so the Self unfolds when the ego breaks and disappears. When a conducive atmosphere is created, the potential tree within the seed will begin to feel the discomfort of being imprisoned in the shell. It longs to come out into the light and to be free. It is the intense urge of the dormant tree within that breaks the shell open. There is pain involved in this breaking of the outer shell. But that pain is nothing in relation to the glory of the manifested tree. Once the seedling emerges, the shell becomes insignificant. Similarly, once Self-Realization is attained, the ego loses all its significance.

"Son, if you believe that the ego is so precious, you may keep it. But your turn will come. Your closed heart, your ego, cannot remain closed forever—it must open up. However, no force can be used for this opening to take place.

"Don't think that the world will disappear once you become egoless, once the bud of the ego has been transformed into the flower of Self-Realization. The world will remain as it is. But you will see it differently. A new world opens up before you—a world of wonders and heavenly beauty will be uncovered within you.

"Within the bud of the ego it is dark and narrow. When the bud gives way and the flower emerges, everything becomes beautiful and pervaded by the most glorious light. You come out of the dark into the radiant light, from imprisonment to freedom, from ignorance to true knowledge. This world of diversity is transformed into perfect oneness. It happens within you, not externally."

IT JUST HAPPENS
IN THE TRUE MASTER'S PRESENCE

Question: "Amma, you said that this opening up cannot be forced. What, then, does the Master do for this opening up to happen?"

Mother: "A true Master is a *presence*, the presence of Divine Consciousness. He does nothing. In his presence everything just happens, without any effort on his part. There can only be effort where there is an ego. A true Master is egoless. There is therefore no effort involved from his side. Even the situations that allow the seeker to dive into his own consciousness arise in the presence of the Master. That is simply how it is—it cannot be otherwise. The sun doesn't make any effort to create its light; yet the sun cannot do anything but shine. A flower doesn't make any effort to be fragrant; being fragrant is just part of its nature. A river doesn't make any effort to flow; it simply flows. It is all so natural. Human beings create unnatural things, but nature can only be natural. Likewise, the perfect Master doesn't do anything in particular to create a suitable situation for your progress. His very presence makes what is needed happen spontaneously. There is no effort involved on his part. His presence is the most conducive atmosphere for the opening of your heart to take place. That is how it is.

"The sun doesn't do anything in particular to make a lotus flower bloom. The sun simply shines in the sky, and by its mere existence, all the lotuses in the ponds and lakes on earth open up. The sun is not doing anything—it just shines. There is no effort involved. Similarly, the presence of a perfect Master is like the radiant sun that makes the lotus of our heart blossom. There is no question of force. His infinitely loving and compassionate presence has the power to melt the rock of the ego. The ego melts and a flow of supreme love is created. The Master is not doing anything.

"Huge ice blocks melt in the heat of the sun. The masses of ice on the Himalayan peaks melt and run down into the valleys. They become rivers and streams where people can drink and bathe. The Satguru's presence can easily melt our rocklike egos and create a wonderful flow of universal love and compassion.

"There is no effort involved in the Master's presence. He is simply there. In his divine presence everything happens spontaneously. The earth doesn't force anything upon us, nor does the sun, the moon, the stars, or anything in nature. Everything simply is. Only selfish, egotistic human beings try to force things on each other.

"As long as you are identified with your body, you will try to force things; but once you go beyond the body you cannot force anything. Once you go beyond the body, once you become bodiless, it means that you are egoless. Using force then becomes impossible.

"Because of the presence of the sun in the sky, countless things happen on earth. The sun is the source of the energy necessary for creation to exist. Without the sun and its rays, humans, animals, and plants could not exist. But the sun is not forcing anything on anyone. The sun is—and by its mere existence everything just happens.

"It is the same with a perfect Master. The sun that we see in the sky is just a small manifestation of the infinite Consciousness. The power of the sun is a minuscule fraction of the entire cosmic energy. The Master, however, is *Purnam* (the Whole). He is that infinite Consciousness itself. Whatever is needed for human evolution happens automatically in his presence. He doesn't need to use any force.

"A perfect Master is the totality of all life, manifested in a human form. In his presence you experience life in all its intensity and vibrancy."

Everyone was deeply absorbed and attentive as Mother spoke. It was as if the Fountain of Knowledge was flowing from its very source, like the holy Ganges flowing down from the Himalayan peaks to the valleys below, letting everyone bathe in its sweet, sacred waters. Sitting still and gazing at Mother's radiant face, everyone gradually went into deep meditation. Only later, when Mother began singing a kirtan did they become aware of their surroundings. Mother sang the song, *Kodanukoti*, creating blissful waves of supreme love.

> *O Eternal Truth,*
> *For millions of years*
> *Mankind has been searching for You.*
>
> *The ancient sages renounced everything,*
> *And for the purpose of making the Self flow,*
> *Through meditation,*
> *Into Your Divine Stream,*
> *They performed endless years of austerities.*
>
> *Your infinitesimal Flame,*
> *Inaccessible to all,*
> *Shines like the blaze of the sun;*
> *It stands perfectly still, without a flutter*
> *In the fierce wind of a cyclone.*
>
> *The flowers and creepers,*
> *The shrine rooms and temples,*
> *With their newly installed sacred pillars,*
> *Have been waiting for You for eons*
> *And still You remain unreachable.*

Mother sat in silence for some time looking up at the sky, and then She continued her sweet, profound conversation.

LOVE CAN ONLY EXIST
WHERE THERE IS NO FORCE

"True life—real, meaningful living, has almost disappeared from the face of the earth. Human beings and the entire society have become mechanical and unfeeling. Bargaining and competition is prevalent everywhere. It can be found even in the family, where there ought to be an atmosphere of deep love and concern, and where life is meant to be experienced in all its fullness. Man, in his selfishness and greed, and his lack of love and compassion, has turned into a heartless machine, familiar only with forcing and imposing.

"The mechanical mind of man likes to use force. We have grown accustomed to selfishness, competition, anger, hatred, jealousy and war. Our familiarity with love is only superficial. We are more familiar with the negative tendencies and know only how to force and impose. Force, however, will destroy all possibilities for love to grow.

"Only anger and hatred can force. Take war for example. War is an extreme way of using force. War is the sum total of anger, hatred, revenge, and all the negative feelings of a population. When the collective mind of a country erupts like a volcano, we call it war. Countries at war try to force their ideas and conditions on each other.

"Love cannot force, for love is the presence of Pure Consciousness. And that presence cannot force—it simply is.

"Real love is experienced when there are no conditions. To have conditions is to force. But where love is present, nothing can be forced. Conditions exist only where there is division. Force is used where there is duality, a sense of 'you and I.' You use force because you perceive the other to be different from you. But force cannot take place when there is only One. The very idea of force disappears in that state. Then you simply are. The universal life force flows through you; you become an open passage. You let the Supreme Consciousness take charge of you. You remove whatever has been obstructing the flow; you remove the self-created bund allowing the river of all-embracing Love to run its course.

"It is as if you have locked yourself in a room for a long time; and now, at last, you open all the doors and windows. You have been complaining, saying, 'Why is there no sunshine in this room? And why is there no breeze in here?' But now you realize what it was that obstructed the light and the breeze. The sun was always shining and the wind was always blowing. They never stopped. As you sat inside the room with all the doors and windows closed, you kept complaining and you blamed the sun and the wind for staying away from you. Now you realize that the fault lay entirely with yourself, and not with the sun or the wind. So you open up the doors and windows allowing the wind and the light to stream in.

"When you open up, you will find that the sun was always shining and the wind was always blowing, carrying the sweet fragrance of Divinity. There are no conditions and no force is being used. You just allow the door of your heart to open up, the door that was never locked. It has always been open, but in your ignorance you thought it was locked.

"The common expression is, 'I love you.' But, instead of 'I love you,' it would be better to say, 'I am love—I am the embodiment of Pure Love.' Remove the I and you, and you will find that there is only Love. It is as if Love is imprisoned between the I and you. Remove the I and you, for they are unreal; they are self-imposed walls that don't exist. The gulf between I and you is the ego. When the ego is removed the distance disappears and the I and you also disappear. They merge to become one—and that is Love. You lend the I and you their reality. Withdraw your support and they will disappear. Then you will realize, not that 'I love you,' but that 'I *am* that all-embracing love.'

"Children, whenever you go through a difficult time in life, think to yourselves: 'I don't expect any love from others, because I am not someone who needs to be loved by others. I am Love itself. I am an inexhaustible source of love, who will always continue to give love, and nothing but love, to everyone who comes to me.'

"A perfect Master's presence is the presence of Divine Love. Divine Love cannot force—it is simply there, for our benefit. Not even worldly love can be forced; what, then, can be said about Divine Love, which is beyond all limitations?

"When two lovers meet and fall in love, they don't talk about terms or conditions before they begin to love each other. If any such exchange were to take place, love couldn't happen. When the lovers see each other their hearts spontaneously overflow; they are irresistibly drawn to each other. There is no force or effort involved, no words or conditions. Love happens when you don't force anything, when you are fully present without any sense of 'I and mine' blocking the flow. The slightest use of force will destroy the beauty of love, so that love cannot happen."

CHAPTER NINE

FEEL THE PAIN OF THOSE WHO SUFFER

*T*his morning during darshan, a woman devotee, who looked as if she was very poor, prayed to Mother with tears in Her eyes, "Amma, there is a terrible poultry disease spreading throughout my village, and my own hens have caught the disease. Amma, please save them!"

A brahmachari who was sitting next to Mother didn't like this. He thought, "What a silly complaint! It is such a crowded day; instead of leaving the hut as soon as they have offered their prostrations to Mother, why do people have to trouble Mother by talking about such trivial things?" As the thought flashed through his mind, Mother who had been busy consoling the woman, gave the brahmachari a stern look and said, "Learn to understand the sorrows and the feelings of others." The brahmachari turned pale. He was stunned when he realized how instantaneously Mother could catch him by reading his thoughts.

Mother in Her spontaneous and affectionate way consoled the woman. She gave her sacred ash to put on her sick hens. The woman smiled relieved and, having received Mother's darshan, she happily left the hut.

When the woman was gone, Mother turned to the brahmachari and said, "Son, you cannot understand the suffering of that daughter. Do you know anything about the difficulties and the afflictions people go through in this world? If you did, you wouldn't have considered her complaint to be silly or insignificant. You have never known the sorrows of life. Only if you yourself have experienced suffering, will you be able to understand that daughter's concern about her hens. Her only way of earning a livelihood is by selling the eggs of those hens. If they die, her family will starve. Those hens are everything to her—they are her entire wealth. When Amma thinks about the hard life that woman leads, She cannot think of that woman's concerns as being insignificant in any way. With the little money she manages to save from the sale of her eggs, she visits Amma once or twice a month. Because Amma is aware of her difficulties, the Ashram sometimes provides her with the bus fare. She has a difficult life, but look at her self-surrender and her love for Amma. Try to see and learn from her simplicity and innocence. When Amma thinks of such people, Amma's heart melts and She finds it difficult to control Her tears. Those who have always had plenty of food to appease their hunger cannot comprehend the hunger of a starving person.

"You know, son, there are three types of people in this

world. There are those who have nothing; then there are
those who are just scraping by; and the third type are those
who have far more than they need. Now, if those who belong to the third category don't do anything to help those of
the first two categories, then Amma would say that those
who belong to the third category, who are supposed to be
rich, are, in fact, the poorest of the poor. Those who have
far more than they need should have eyes with which to see
the suffering of others; they should have ears to hear the
distressed calls for help; they should have a loving heart with
which to feel compassion towards those who suffer, and they
should have willing hands with which to lend their assis-
tance to those in need. Children, listen to the desperate calls
for help! No one's pain is insignificant. In order to really
hear their sorrow-stricken words you need to have a compassionate heart, a heart that enables you to see and to feel
the suffering of others as if it were your own. Try to come
down to their level and feel the vibrations of their aching
hearts. If you cannot do this, then all the spiritual practices
you do are a useless waste."

On hearing Mother's powerful words the brahmachari was
full of remorse. With tears in his eyes he sought forgiveness
for the mistake he had committed.

Since the beginning of darshan, a young man had been

looking intently at Mother. He was a college lecturer from Nagpur. The day he had arrived at the Ashram he had been in a hurry and had said, "I'm just going to have Mother's darshan and then I'm leaving. I have some urgent things to do as soon as I get back to Nagpur." But several days had now gone by, and he was still at the Ashram. Mother said to the other devotees, "Everyday he comes and tells Amma, 'I am leaving today,' and everyday Amma gives him permission to go. Amma says to him, "Okay, son, you go and come back.' But he never leaves."

The college lecturer, who didn't speak Malayalam, didn't understand what Mother was talking about. But because everyone was looking at him, he guessed that Mother was talking about him. A devotee came to his aid and translated what Mother had just said. He responded, "I am not going at all. Then what to say about going and coming back?"

Mother smilingly replied, "But Amma also knows the trick of chasing you away."

Everybody laughed.

As the darshan continued, the brahmacharis sang *Prema Prabho Lasini. . .*

> O Goddess
> Enjoyer of immortal bliss

Who revels in the brilliance of Love
And from whose flowerlike smile
The light of bliss pours forth. . .

You are the One
Who, with the waves of the River
Of Immortal Bliss
Caress those who are searching for the path
Of a life untouched by the fear of sin.

Your Lotus Feet
Richly enveloped by the light
Of the Supreme Self,
Are granting auspiciousness
By destroying the bondage of Becoming.

May You cast that indestructible Light on me
Whose heart bows down to You
That I may merge in the Universal Soul.

THE FEELING OF BONDAGE

A brahmachari asked a question. "Amma, the scriptures say that the sense of 'I and you' is unreal, that it is a self-imposed wall that doesn't exist, and that we ourselves lend it its reality. If it is unreal, and if everything is one, why, then, am I feeling the difference?"

Mother: "It is your ignorance about your oneness with the

Whole that causes the difference. In reality, there is no
bondage, there is no wall separating you from your divine
nature. The wall, or bondage, is an illusion created by the
mind. Remove the illusion, and your mind will simultaneously
be removed.

"There was a cowherd boy who took the cows to the
meadows every morning and brought them back to the cow
shed in the evening. Before he left for the night, he made
sure that all the cows were properly tied to their posts. One
evening, he found that one of the cows was missing its rope.
The boy was in a fix. He couldn't leave the cow untied as
she would probably run away and get lost, and as it was already dark, it was too late to go and buy a new rope. The
boy went to the monk who was in charge of the place, and
sought his advice. The monk said to him, 'It is nothing to
worry about. Just go back to the cow, stand next to her and
pretend that you are tying her. Make sure that the cow sees
you doing it, and that will be enough. The cow will stay were
she is.'

"The boy went back to the cow shed and did as the monk
had told him. He pretended that he was tying the cow to
the post. When the boy returned the next morning, he found
to his amazement that the cow had remained absolutely still
throughout the night. The boy untied all the cows as usual

and was about to go to the meadows, when he noticed that the cow with the missing rope was still lying down next to the post. He tried to coax her back to the herd, but she wouldn't budge. The boy was perplexed. He once again went to seek the monk's advice. The monk listened to the boy and smiled. 'Look, my child,' he said, 'the cow still thinks that she is bound to the post. Yesterday when the rope was missing, you pretended that you were tying her. This morning you untied all the cows except this particular one. You thought it wasn't necessary as she wasn't actually tied up. But because of your little act last night, the cow still believes that she is tied to the post. So now you have to go back and pretend that you are setting her free.' The boy returned to the cow and pretended to untie her. The cow immediately got up and ran off to join the herd.

"We are in a similar situation. The bondage, or the wall of separation, is self-created. The wall has been created by the ego, but the ego is also unreal—it is an illusion that has no existence of its own. It appears to be real because of the power it derives from the Atman. It is animated by the Atman. The ego can be compared to dead matter, for without the Self it is insentient. Stop giving any importance to the ego. Learn to ignore it. It will then withdraw and disappear. We give the unreal ego its reality. Expose it and that will be the end of it.

"Due to our ignorance, we believe that we are bound just like the cow, when, if fact, we are completely free. We need to be convinced of this, however. When our ignorance about our true being, our freedom, is removed, the bondage also disappears.

"Amma knows a man who was in chains for a long time. He was totally insane and had to stay in a mental hospital. Finally, he was brought home. But they had to lock him in a room, with his hands tied behind his back. His hands were tied like that because he often became violent and would attack people. After many years of treatment he finally re-covered. But even today one can see that he always keeps his hands behind his back as if they were tied there. When Amma met him, he told Her that after all this time he con-tinues to feel as if his hands were tied behind his back. Whenever someone offers him a cup of tea, or when he is about to eat, his mind finds it difficult to move his hands. It takes a few seconds for him to realize that his hands are no longer tied behind his back. Occasionally, others have to remind him that his hands are free. His hands are free, but he needs to be reminded of it. There is no real bondage; there is only a self-imposed bondage.

"It is the same with us. As long as there is a feeling of bondage, we need the help of a perfect Master who can show us the way and say to us, 'Look, you are not bound at all. You are the all-powerful Atman, the Self. Come out of the illusion and soar up through the skies of Supreme Consciousness.' The Master pretends that he is untying the rope that binds you to the post of worldly objects and pleasures. Once the illusion is removed, you realize that you were always in that Consciousness, that you have never, ever strayed from it.

"A perfect Master's guidance and his presence is the light that illumines your path. His presence helps you to see the self-created wall of the ego. By understanding the illusory nature of your bondage, it can easily be removed. Your wrong understanding about your relationship with people, with the world, and the objects of the world, creates the bondage."

A UNITY - NOT A RELATIONSHIP

Question: "Amma, are you saying that relationships cause that bondage?"

Mother: "Yes, a relationship does create bondage, if one doesn't have the proper understanding and discrimination. But the truth is that a relationship can only exist as long as there is a perception of there being two. Once the realization of the Self arises, there can be no question of a relationship, because the two disappear. From that point onwards, there is only oneness, and total detachment.

"When all feelings of duality disappear, all relationships also disappear. Two individuals, families, or nations can have a relationship; but when everything is One, there can no longer be a relationship. Then, there is only One, an all-encompassing awareness. Relationships bind, whereas perfect awareness of the Self frees you from all bondage. In a relationship you are like a caged bird. Realization of the Self lets you out of the cage of the ego and sets you free.

"The body and its different parts, though seemingly different, are one, a unity. The hands, legs, eyes, nose, ears, and all the internal organs, are part of the whole. It is a unity, one body—not a relationship. Similarly, the branches, leaves, flowers and fruits of a tree are all parts of the one whole tree. You cannot call it a relationship.

"When the self-created wall of the ego is lifted, you will realize that the dualistic nature of the world is only an external appearance, and that, in essence, everything is a whole, a single unity.

"The outer world is given far too much importance, while the inner world is ignored. This will only serve to increase the density of our ignorance. If we lay to much emphasis on our relationship with the outer world, while we ignore the inner world, it will increase the gap between us and our true Self."

Mother stopped talking and asked the brahmacharis to sing. They sang *Sukhamenni Tirayunna...*

> *You, who are searching*
> *For happiness everywhere,*
> *How will you find it*
> *Without shedding your vanity?*
> *Until the compassionate One,*
> *The Mother of the Universe,*
> *Shines within your heart*
> *How can you be happy?*
>
> *The mind*
> *In which devotion towards Shakti,*
> *The Supreme Power,*
> *Is not alive*
> *Is like a flower without fragrance.*
>
> *Such a mind will be forced*
> *To toss about in misery*
> *Like a leaf*
> *Tossed by the waves*
> *Of the restless ocean.*
>
> *Do not get caught in the talons*
> *Of the vulture known as fate*
> *Worship the Self in seclusion*

Stop expecting the fruits
Of your actions
Worship the form of the Universal Self
In the blossom of your heart.

DON'T BLAME THE CIRCUMSTANCES

When the song had come to an end, Mother continued to talk.

"The natural tendency in human beings is to find fault with the situations in life. We always complain about the circumstances, blaming the world for our sorrows, suffering and fear. This habit of ours to complain and find fault with the outside world, and the circumstances it creates, is due to our ignorance of our true being, that we are the Self (Atman). The Atman is beyond all limitations, untouched by anything that happens to us, whether good or bad.

"A man was strolling in a mango grove. Suddenly a rotten mango fell with a splash on his bald head. His head was covered with the juice of rotten mango; it even trickled down his cheeks. The man was furious and began cursing the mango and the mango tree, and also the bird who had pecked it down; above all, he showered curses on the law of gravity itself! Wouldn't it be foolish to do such a thing? We would make a laughing stock of ourselves. But seen from a higher level of consciousness, this is exactly what we are doing.

"If we take the above example and think for a moment, we will find that the situation, in itself, clearly can't be blamed. Wouldn't it be absurd to curse the law of gravity? Or the tree and the bird? How is the law of gravity supposed to change? Whether rotten or not, a mango cannot fall upwards. It has to fall down because that is the law of nature. When mangoes are ripe they either fall from the tree of their own accord, or they are sometimes pecked down by a bird. No one, with even a little intelligence, would lay any blame for this. To view the situation in that way would clearly be wrong. Once we perceive this in a deeper, more subtle way, and learn to accept the situations in life, rather than fight against them, we will discover that life is extremely beautiful.

"Do not blame the circumstances and do not blame others. Remove your own weaknesses. Your failures and your hurt feelings, your fears and your troubles, are all due to some weakness within yourself, and this weakness is known as ignorance. You identify with your thoughts which are based on a misconception.

"The following story will be helpful in understanding the illusory nature of the world. After having performed the *rajasuya yajna* (the royal festival of charity), the Pandavas invited their cousin, Duryodhana, and his brothers to stay at Indraprastha, the royal abode of the Pandavas, for a few more days, to which Duryodhana agreed. One day they were looking at the beautiful palace, which had been very skillfully designed. In one of the halls the floor was so polished and transparent, it was made to look like a small lake with gleaming ripples on the surface. Duryodhana and his brothers were so deluded by this that they got undressed intending to swim across the lake. When Draupadi and Bhima saw this they laughed, because there was no lake or any water there.

"In another palace they thought the floor looked like any ordinary floor and began to walk on it without a moment's hesitation. But that spot was, in fact, a lake, though it didn't look like one. The brothers just walked out onto it and fell with a splash into the water. They were completely drenched. The whole place was so cleverly designed that Duryodhana and his brothers were totally deluded.

"This can be compared to the world. The entire world has been so fantastically designed and decorated by the Creator that, if we don't move cautiously, we are easily deluded. Each step should be taken with alertness.

"Some places, situations, and experiences may look normal, harmless and wonderful. But look carefully, be watchful, because what you see on the surface may be just a cover. The beauty and charm may be only skin deep; just behind that beautifully decorated cover great danger may be lurking.

"Another place, situation, or experience may seem dangerous. You may create a hue and a cry and take all sorts of precautions if you are forced to face it. But it could turn out to be something very normal, and even constructive. Such things happen in life. We are fooled and deceived more than a thousand times, and yet, we don't learn our lesson. Even after countless deceptions, people continue to run after all sorts of things. This is the extraordinary power of *Maya*.

"The world is not the problem. The problem lies within ourselves. So be watchful, and you will see things with greater clarity. Watchfulness provides you with a penetrating eye and mind, so that you cannot be deceived. It will slowly take you closer to your true being, the bliss of the Atman.

"Bliss is our true nature, not sorrow. But something has happened to us. Everything has been turned upside down. Happiness has become a 'strange' mood while sorrow is considered to be natural.

"There is an old musician who frequently visits the Ashram. He is a very happy man, always laughing, telling jokes, and moving freely with people. He is always joyful. When people see how happy he is, they accuse him of being mentally abnormal. Amma knows this son well. He is perfectly all right, a good-hearted soul. But his joy is strange to others. If somebody is happy, people immediately become suspicious. They want to know why the person looks so happy, as if it were something unnatural. Only when we are sad are we believed to be 'normal.' That is why Amma says that everything has been turned upside down. What a pity! People, who are essentially joyful and harmonious, believe that happiness is unnatural, and that the only natural state is pain and sorrow."

As the darshan was coming to a close, the brahmacharis sang another song, *Asa Nasi Katora.* . .

> *O mind,*
> *You are a busy harbor of desires*
> *Constantly buffeted by their flow.*
> *Beware, don't drown*
> *In the deep ocean of sorrow*
> *Do arati to the Atman instead;*
> *Keep your attention focused on the Self.*
>
> *Beware,*
> *If you continue in this way*
> *Without any real support*
> *You will fall in the end*
> *And be full of remorse.*
>
> *If you cherish Eternal Bliss,*
> *If you covet Liberation,*
> *Then meditate*
> *O mind, meditate on your Source.*

Meditate on the inner Ocean of Bliss
Give up your demonic qualities
And follow the teachings of the Divine chants.

CHAPTER TEN

A HEALING TOUCH

A young man was sitting on the verandah of the old temple, with his head resting between his knees. Mother happened to walk by, and when She saw him sitting there She went up to him. The young man, lost in thought, was not aware of Mother's presence. Mother lovingly tapped him on his shoulder saying, "Son." The man looked up and was startled to see the Holy Mother standing in front of him. There was a look of deep agony in his eyes. Mother smiled at him, gently tapped his chest and said, "Anger. . . anger is poison. You should control it." There was obvious shock on his face. He covered his face with his hands and started weeping. Mother looked at him and Her motherly affection overflowed. She gently put his head on Her shoulder and caressed him saying, "Son, don't worry! Everything will be all right. Amma will take care of everything."

The man had a very bad temper, and on that particular day he had had a big fight with his wife. Finally his parents interfered. They supported his wife knowing that she was an innocent victim of his frequent attacks. The interference of his parents accelerated his anger. He shouted at them and behaved disrespectfully. This was not an isolated incident. Due to his uncontrollable anger such scenes were quite common in the house. He always regretted his mistake afterwards and ended up apologizing to his wife and parents. But again and again he found himself helplessly plunged into his terrible moods. Finally, after the incident on this particular day, his neighbors, who were devotees of Mother, advised him to go and meet Her. That is how he came to see Mother. Now he is a completely changed person. The same man who, because of his uncontrollable anger, was a terror to his family, is now a loving and caring husband, son, and father. The whole family visits Amma to seek Amma's blessings at least once a week.

He said, "After that first touch of Mother's on my chest, I felt that something very heavy had been lifted away from my heart. That touch removed the poison of anger within me. Before this, my family life had been a nightmare. Now, by Mother's Grace, my home has been transformed into an abode of peace and happiness. My whole family has become Mother's devotees."

Countless similar incidents have happened around Mother. Millions of lives have been transformed by Her Grace. But though She is a great transformer of lives and a healer of hearts, Mother remains a wonderful example of utter humility and simplicity.

HOW TO OVERCOME FEAR

At about four o'clock in the afternoon, while everyone was sitting in front of the old temple, a young lawyer asked Mother a question. "Amma, fear seems to be taken for granted as being part of human existence. People are afraid of everything: their job, the security of the family, fear of others and of society. Man has created a whole world of fear around him. How could this happen? What causes it, and how can we overcome these fears, which gnaw away at all the beauty of life from within?"

Mother: "We again come back to ignorance. Ignorance about our true existence in God, or the Atman, is the cause of all sorts of fear. The outer life of a human being—whatever he does for the sake of his bodily existence—should be lived in concordance with his inner existence. There should be a perfect balance. If man gives more importance to his body, as he is doing now, and neglects his soul, he becomes worried and anxious, fervently clinging to false securities.

"There was a great Master who was worshipped by hundreds of thousands of people from all over the world. People were amazed at his purity, his innocence, and the depth of his wisdom. He transformed many lives through the beauty of his teachings and the love and compassion he manifested.

Out of curiosity his disciples and devotees used to ask him to reveal the source of his knowledge and his purity. But the Master would only say to them, 'It's all contained in the book you will inherit when I leave this body.'

"One day the Master left his body. A few days later his disciples began to search for the book he had mentioned, and they found it. But there was only one page between the covers of the book and only a single sentence written on it. This is what it said: 'Dear ones, know the difference between the container and the content, and true knowledge will dawn within you, dispelling all fear and darkness.'

"Children, the secret lies in knowing that the body is the container, and that the content, the soul, is different from the container. The milk is different from the vessel in which it is contained. The vessel is not the milk, and the milk is not the vessel. Self-knowledge will eliminate all the unnecessary fears that grip our lives.

"As human beings we want food, clothing and shelter. This is understandable. These three things are the main concerns of our body, and we are anxious to make the body comfortable. But what is this body? Where does it come from? What is the power that manifests through this body, making you love it so much? Few consider this, and are concerned about it. People believe that the body is everything, that there is nothing beyond their bodily existence. This attitude makes them extremely attached to the body and its security.

"Your attachment to the body causes fear concerning everything in your life. As your attachment to the body increases, the ego also increases, with the simultaneous increase of your fear. Attachment to the body makes you attached to the ego, because you believe that your body is the most precious thing you have. You want to protect it from anything that could harm it in any way. You think your bodily security is the only safety in existence. What a pity that is! We do not understand that the existence of the body depends on the soul.

"The nature of both body and soul needs to be properly understood. The body is constantly subject to change, whereas the soul is immutable. Without the immutable soul as its substratum, the mutable body could not exist. The ever changing body is perishing, whereas the changeless soul is imperishable. The imperishable soul is the life force; it is the taproot supporting the tree of the body.

"Our problem is that we give too much importance to the external, manifested body and completely ignore the unmanifested Self, the source of our existence. We may try to reason with ourselves saying, 'I see only the body and not the soul, which is why I give so much importance to the body. How can I believe in a soul that is invisible?' But this is like saying, 'I can only see the tree, so how am I to believe in the root which is invisible to my naked eye?' No person with even a little bit of intelligence would make such a statement.

"Say that you are looking out across an immense ocean. You are thrilled by what you see and you think, 'How wonderful that infinite ocean is! It is so inconceivably deep and vast.' But you can only see the surface—you cannot see the world that exists beneath the surface, and you cannot see its underlying ground. Wouldn't it be unwise if you were to say that the world beneath the surface, and the bottom of the ocean do not exist, just because they happen to be invisible from where you are standing? The very existence of the surface of the ocean is enough to prove the existence of the underlying ground. Without the substratum to support it, the sea could not exist. Even without the water, the ground exists.

"In order to see and experience the world beneath the ocean and its underlying ground, you have to go beneath the surface. You have to dive deep into the ocean. In a similar way, to realize the soul one has to go beyond the body and penetrate deep into one's own Self.

"Just as we feel a sense of amazement when we look at the vastness of the ocean in this way, if we could only feel the same sense of awe and wonder when we look at all of Nature and her infinite manifestations, we would never be skeptical about the inner life force existing as the one Substratum of the manifested world.

"Man's fear is due to his ignorance about his own soul, the life force and substratum of his existence. He believes that he should worry only about his physical existence, that life is all about the body, and nothing else. This is his concept about life—indeed, his whole life is built around this misunderstanding. Once he gives all his attention to the body and the ego, the next step is his security. He builds a fortress of false securities around him. He clings to his house because that is a form of security; his job or business is another; his status in society is yet another; then comes his family and his countless possessions. He thinks that life consists of clinging to these external 'securities,' that without them, and without his body and ego, there is no existence. For him the whole of life can be put into two words: 'body' and 'attachments.' But it is not his fault; for, to him, existence is the same as the existence of the body, and for the sake of his body he needs all those false securities. Poor man, he has completely forgotten the inner life.

"Real life is developed from within. Real living means that the soul expresses itself through all one's thoughts, words, and actions. A person becomes fearless once he understands the nature of the imperishable soul.

"At this stage, however, he is only familiar with the perishable body, which makes him increasingly afraid and pushes him more and more towards death, which is his greatest fear.

"Death will grab everything, all that he has and that he claims as his own. Death is the greatest threat to a human being. Nobody wants to die. The very mention of death causes tremendous fear. But death is an experience like any other."

When Mother speaks, Her words take wing as if they were about to soar up, carrying the listener along with them. Her words and expressions never sound as if they are coming from a person, from an individual. They resonate as if emerging out of a deep cave, from an ancient, unknown source. Mother's words act as a vehicle that carries the listener to the deeper realms of the spiritual world.

Mother began to sing the song, *Marikkatta Manushyarundo…*

> *Is there anyone who will not die?*
> *Is there a moment when desire ends?*
> *We are born on this earth*
> *We are scorched by sorrow*

And then we die
To be reborn again.

Though man learns to laugh
What greatness has he
If he is afraid of death?

Though born as a human being
What glory is there to a human life
If the fear of death doesn't leave?

Everything happens as decided by destiny
But who creates that destiny?
This world can never lead to happiness.
Once we realize this truth
We will renounce everything.

CHAPTER ELEVEN

THE ALL-KNOWING MOTHER

*I*t was almost midnight. Mother was strolling in the coconut grove in front of the Ashram. At times She stopped and stood facing east, as if She was waiting for someone to arrive. Bri. Gayatri and the senior brahmacharis suggested several times that Mother go to bed. But Mother politely refused and stayed in the coconut grove. A few minutes past twelve a large family arrived at the Ashram. The entire family were overjoyed when they saw Mother standing in the coconut grove. Mother called them, and having expressed Her love and affection towards them in Her unique motherly way, she began talking to them. The Ashram residents now understood why Mother had remained in the coconut grove and hadn't wanted to go to Her room.

The family had left Quilon at eight o'clock in the evening, hoping they would see Mother if they reached the Ashram by nine, but their car had broken down on the way. By the time a mechanic was found and the car had been repaired, it was very late. They decided to return to Quilon and to visit Mother another day.

But their five year old son was extremely disappointed and repeatedly told them he wanted to see Mother that night. He was so insistent that, finally, the family yielded to his wish and continued driving to the Ashram. They never thought they would be able to see Mother at such a late hour of the night. Their only desire was to spend a few minutes in the Ashram atmosphere and then return to Quilon. But to their great surprise, as they arrived they saw Mother standing in front of the Ashram, as if She were expecting them.

The family had some serious problems. Their aching hearts found much relief by just seeing Mother. The most compassionate Mother talked to them for more than two hours.

At four-thirty in the morning Mother had just taken bath and was again walking outside. She looked fresh and radiant. One of the brahmacharis approached Mother and begged Her, "Amma, why don't You go and rest for some time? Today is a Devi Bhava day, so You won't get any rest tonight either."

"Son," Mother replied, "one shouldn't sleep while the Archana is being performed. That would be setting a bad example. During the morning Archana the whole Ashram should be awake and vibrant with the spiritual energy that is created by the chanting. There shouldn't be any tamasic energy present at that time."

The brahmachari said, "But Amma, You are beyond everything. You are Devi Herself. You are completely detached and untouched by everything."

Mother replied, "Son, if Amma is not up at this time, you won't be either. It would cause discipline problems in the Ashram, and everyone would do whatever they felt like doing. Unless Amma sets an example by practicing what is being preached, nobody will feel inspired to follow the rules."

"But, Amma, if Your body doesn't get any rest, won't Your health suffer?" asked the brahmachari. "You are sacrificing everything for the sake of others. Amma, what can we, Your children, do for You?" The brahmachari was almost in tears as he spoke.

Mother patted him affectionately on the back and said, "Don't worry about Amma." Pointing at Her own body She said, "This will take care of itself. Amma has not come to the world to protect Her body. Amma doesn't care what happens to the body—let it take its natural course. Amma wants to sacrifice everything for the uplift of Her children, and for the benefit of the world. You should strictly follow your daily routine and try to be free from the grip of the ego. That is enough. Son, everything about this body and its existence in the world is decided by Amma. There is a purpose to fulfill. Only when that has been achieved will this body go."

Mother uttered the last three sentences as if She were talking from another world. For some time, the brahmachari just stood there and gazed at the indescribable phenomenon that is Mother; and then he proceeded to the meditation hall where the morning Archana was about to begin.

CHAPTER TWELVE

DEATH IS ONLY A CHANGE

*M*other was sitting with a few brahmacharis be-side the moonlit backwaters. The moon and the stars were strewn like jewels across the blue-black sky.

A brahmachari asked Mother a question. "Amma, what causes the pain and the fear of death?"

Mother: "The pain of death is caused by the thought that death is going to destroy everything that you have—all that you are attached to and all that you cling to. That clinging causes the pain. If only you can let go of all your attach-ments, then the pain of death will turn into an experience of bliss. In death you lose everything that you claim to be yours. All that is dear and wonderful to you—your family, the love and laughter of your near and dear ones, this beau-tiful world with all its precious treasures—everything is go-ing to dissolve and disappear. Just the thought of it shakes your entire being. You want to forget about death because you are afraid that you will enter oblivion and won't exist anymore. It kills your enthusiasm and makes you numb with dread, so you don't want to think about it at all.

Question: "Amma, I have heard You say that death is an experience, like any other. What do you mean by this?"

Mother: "Birth and death are two inevitable experiences. Once you go beyond death you also go beyond birth. A person who can see birth and death as being perfectly natural, just like any other experience in life, will be able to lead a happy and blissful life. He sees the whole of life with all its experiences, both good and bad, as being a play. He won't complain about anything; he cannot find fault with anyone or any situation. Such people will always have a genuine smile on their face, even while confronting the worst situations in life. The words and deeds of others cannot hurt them or make them angry. Being established in a relaxed and composed mood, they enjoy life with the wonder and innocence of a child.

"Just like other joyful moments of life, death can also be a joyful experience. People normally rejoice when a child is born, but they weep when death occurs. Both birth and death are two normal transitions. But this can be known only when one goes beyond the ego and realizes the Self.

"When a child is born, a transition takes place. It doesn't stop there. The child grows; he or she passes through several stages, or passages, of life. The body is transformed from that of a child to a teenager, to a young adult, and then comes middle age and finally old age. The process of transformation continues. Death occurs which is another transformation. This is normal; there is nothing wrong with it. You should learn to see death as a normal transformation just like other changes of the body. Birth is not the beginning of life, nor is death the end. The beginning and end are only relative.

"When a child is born, we think it is the very beginning of life. But life, itself, is neither first nor last, new or old; it never began, nor does it ever end. Life is another name for God. Life, when conditioned by the body, is known as the *jivatman*, and when that same life is devoid of all conditions, it is the *Paramatman*. So life is another name for the Atman, or Brahman. Life is without beginning and without end.

"A new birth is therefore not the beginning of existence. You could call it a fresh start, or yet another chance to continue the onward journey towards the real Source of existence. Being born is like the return of the same contents in a different package.

"Death is not complete annihilation. It is a pause. It is like pressing the pause button on a tape recorder in the middle of a song. Sooner or later, when pressed again, the pause button is released and the song continues. Death is only a period of preparation before the start of another life. You unpack your content only to re-pack it in a fresh new package, in which the ingredients will be the same.

"Life and death are the two major events in life, two intense experiences. Once you realize that birth and death are neither the beginning nor the end, life becomes infinitely beautiful and blissful.

"Experiences keep on changing, but the inner 'Experiencer'—the Self, God, or Life, is immutable. This is the truth which needs to be realized. The Experiencer, that is, the Substratum of all experiences, even that of birth and death, is always the same—it is imperishable and immutable. The Experiencer takes you through all your experiences. This is the truth which cannot be altered by time or space.

"Birth and death are only relative. They are not real from the ultimate viewpoint. Like any experience in life, they are two events that a person is bound to go through. But they are by far the most intense experiences we go through. Because of their intensity, nature has devised a method by which man completely forgets these two major moments of his life. Because of the intensity of these experiences, it is difficult for an ordinary person to remain aware during his own birth and death. Birth and death are two stages of life in which one is utterly helpless. While in the womb and while emerging out of the womb, the child is helpless. It is the same with a dying person. During both of these experiences the ego has receded so far into the background, that it is powerless. Children, you are not aware of what is happening to you during or after death. You have to be fearless and fully aware to be open to the experience. If you are afraid you will be closed to the experience. Only those who have enough depth, who are fearless, and who are constantly in a state of awareness, a state of absolute wakefulness, are able to consciously experience the bliss of death.

"Suppose you have an intense stomach ache. You are then aware of the pain. If water is hot or cold, the body immediately feels it. The sorrow caused by your father's death, or the joy felt when a child is born, is experienced directly by the mind. Also, your intellect immediately reacts to the praise or insults showered upon you by others. Such direct experience of the mind is not available during birth and death. This is the reason why we don't consider birth and death to be ordinary experiences.

"Of course, if you have the capacity to remain conscious and alert while passing through the experience of death, it becomes an ordinary experience like other experiences. Then birth and death do not bother you; you simply smile during both occasions. Death is then no longer a strange experience to you. However, this is possible only if you are at one with your true Self."

Question: "Amma, what is the reason for this absence of direct experience during birth and death?"

Mother: "Lack of awareness is the reason. Our level of awareness is very low. Due to our unwise attachments to the world, which is due to our wrong understanding, we are leading an almost unconscious life, even though we are moving and breathing.

"Once all these attachments are dropped, death will turn out to be a blissful experience. As a result of the realization that you are not the body, but the Supreme Consciousness, the whole center of your existence will be shifted to the Self. You will wake up and realize that you were sleeping, and that the dream which is this world, and all the experiences associated with it, is only a play. You will laugh as you look at this exquisite play of consciousness. You will laugh at all the colors. Just as a child, who is looking at the different colors of a rainbow, laughs and enjoys it with wonder in his eyes, so you will find yourself laughing with joy, and you will continue to laugh, even at the face of death, because death is just another play of colors, a different shade in the rainbow of life.

"Once you attain this state, all experiences such as happiness and sorrow, insult and praise, heat and cold, birth and death, pass right through you. You remain beyond it all, as the 'Experiencer,' the very substratum of all experience, witnessing everything like a playful child.

"Children, learn to do everything consciously. Not even a single breath should escape without you being aware of it. Be conscious of your every movement. This will slowly make you fully aware, even of death.

"To attain the state of complete oneness with the Supreme, one has to lose oneself. This, however, is our greatest fear: that we will lose ourselves. For to lose oneself would be a form of dying, and who wants to die? Everyone wants to live. But in order to live life fully, we must learn to love life at its very essence, and to let go of everything else. Learn to embrace life with open arms as you let go of your attachments. Let go of all that you cling to, all your regrets, all your fears and anxieties. But this letting go is not a loss at all, it is the biggest gain there is. It brings the entire universe to you, and you become God."

CHAPTER THIRTEEN

GIVING INSIGHT TO THE BLIND

A young man who had been blind since birth was staying at the Ashram. Ever since he came, the brahmacharis had been looking after him, taking care of all his needs. They served him food and even assisted him when he had to do his nature calls.

Today, more people than expected came for Mother's darshan. Because of this, the rice and curry which had been cooked for lunch finished very soon, before everyone had eaten. A second round of cooking was underway. Due to the workload, the brahmacharis forgot to fetch the blind man from his room for lunch. As soon as they realized their mistake, one of the brahmacharis rushed to the man's room to fetch him. But the blind man was already coming down the steps with the help of a devotee. The brahmachari apologized and explained what had happened saying, "Kindly forgive me. I was so busy serving in the dining hall that I forgot to come and fetch you."

But the man was not appeased. He was feeling hurt and unhappy. "I have money with me," he said. "I can always get

food from somewhere outside the Ashram if I pay for it."
With these words he returned to his room with the help of
the devotee.

Even though the man was upset, the brahmachari ignored
it, thinking that he had only reacted because he was hungry.
The brahmachari soon returned with some fruits which he
placed in front of the young man. He said to him, "Lunch
will be ready in a few minutes. I will bring your food. In the
mean time, please eat these fruits." But the man was still
angry and bluntly rejected the fruits that were offered to him.

Somehow the news reached Mother, and shortly thereafter, she entered the blind man's room. Looking sternly at
the brahmachari, Mother said, "What sort of shraddha do
you have? Why didn't you serve him his lunch at the right
time? Don't you know that this son is blind and that he cannot
come down by himself? If you thought it would take too much
time to fetch him, you should have brought a plate to his
room. If you don't feel compassion towards those who are
helpless, like this son, what is the point of doing spiritual
practices?

"Children, don't miss a single opportunity you get to serve
others. Nobody should have to wait patiently to receive our
help according to our own convenience. In offices and other
work places, people do their duty according to the schedule.

They get remuneration for the work they do, which is why they work. But a sadhak's (spiritual aspirant's) whole life is dedicated to serving others. The reward is not received in terms of a monthly salary. You receive your reward in the form of mental purity and God's Grace. Because you are not getting any immediate remuneration, you shouldn't feel that it is any less important or that your work can be postponed a little. Every opportunity to serve others must be utilized to the maximum, and the work should be done with utmost love and diligence. Only then does it become real worship. True service is to assist those who are helpless, and to make the effort to understand their needs and their feelings."

Mother stroked the blind man's back and asked him, "Son, were you sad? The brahmacharis were very busy in the dining hall; that is why they couldn't fetch you at the right time. Also, the brahmachari who usually helps you is not here today. He entrusted the job to another brahmachari, who is in charge of serving the food in the dining hall. Don't think it was done on purpose. Son, you should learn to be more flexible and adapt to the circumstances wherever you are. Patience is needed in an ashram. As long as you are here, you should be prepared to make a little sacrifice now and then. In that way you will receive God's Grace.

"Son, your blindness is not really a problem. Remember

that you are closer to God, to your true Self, than most people with external eyes. It is true that you cannot see the world, but you can feel God more than a person with normal eyesight, provided you have the right understanding and shraddha. A person with external eyes moves far away from God, from his true nature, the Atman, because he travels too much through the world of objects. So, don't think you are unlucky. Learn to adjust to life. Have more forbearance and patience. That will certainly help you to experience God's presence, both within and without. Son, there are millions of people who are plunged into utter sorrow and despair, even though they have eyes with which to see the world. But there are also people who are happy and contented, even though they cannot see. Surdas, the great devotee of Lord Krishna, had no eyesight; but he led a totally contented life, because he was wise enough to understand the essential principle of life. Through his love and devotion to the Lord, he developed the inner eye, which made him completely blissful, even without his external eyes."

The young man shed tears as he listened to Mother's words. He sobbed like a small child. The brahmacharis and some of the devotees present, couldn't control their tears either. Such was the intense love animating Mother's words.

Affectionately rubbing the young man's back and wiping away his tears with her hands, Mother inquired, "Son, did you eat anything?" He shook his head and said with a choked voice, "But I am satisfied just by Your presence and by listening to Your words. I don't feel hungry at all anymore. My heart is so full with the joy of Your nectarous words."

Mother asked the brahmachari to bring him a plate of food. When he came back with a plate filled with rice and curry, Mother made the blind man sit down next to Her, and She began feeding him with her own hands. Mother fed him with balls of rice, just like a mother would feed her small child, patiently waiting for him as he slowly swallowed the food. In this way, She fed him the entire plate of rice. Those who witnessed this scene were deeply moved as they beheld the pure, divine love which was flowing out of Mother. Softly, everyone began to sing *Kannilengillum*. . .

> *Today I have seen my darling Krishna,*
> *The Beloved of Radha,*
> *Not with these eyes*
> *But with the inner eye.*
>
> *I have seen the Stealer of the mind,*
> *Beauty personified,*
> *The Divine Musician;*
> *I have seen my Lord of Oneness.*

Was He as blue as the ocean?
Did He have a peacock feather
Adorning His curly locks?
I cannot say
But I have seen His gracious form
Through the sound of His Flute.

GLOSSARY

ARATI: Vespers, waving the burning camphor, which leaves
   no residue, with ringing of bells at the end of worship,
   representing the complete offering of the ego to God.

BHAJAN: Devotional singing.

BHAVA SAMADHI: Absorption of the mind into God through
devotion.

DARSHAN: Audience of a holy person or deity.

DEVI MAHATMYAM: An ancient text in praise of the
   Divine Mother.

DHARMA: Righteousness, in accordance with Divine Harmony.

GURUKULA: A Guru's ashram cum school where students
   gain a foundation in spiritual and worldly knowledge
   through study and service.

JIVATMAN: The individual soul.

LEELA: A divine play or show, appearance.

MAHABHARATA: An epic of ancient India, written by the
   sage Vyasa about the family fight between the Pandavas
   and the Kauravas, both cousins of Lord Krishna, which
   culminated in a catastrophic war.

MAHATMA: Great Soul or Sage.

MAYA: Illusion.

MOKSHA: Release from the cycle of birth and death.

MUDRA: Hand pose indicative of mystic truths.

NARAYANEEYAM: The story of Lord Krishna's life written
   by the great devotee Narayana Bhattatiri of Kerala.

PADA PUJA: Worship of the feet of God or a saint.

PARAMATMAN: The Supreme Soul or God.

PRASAD: Consecrated offerings distributed at the end of worship.

PURNAM: Full or perfect.

RAJASUYA YAGNA: A Vedic sacrifice performed by kings.

RAMAYANA: The epic story of Lord Rama, written by the sage Valmiki.

RISHIS: The seers of ancient times to whom Divine Knowledge was revealed and who transmitted it to their disciples.

SADHAK: A spiritual aspirant.

SADHANA: Spiritual practice.

SAKSHI BHAVA: The attitude of being a witness.

SAMADHI: Absorption of the mind into Reality or Truth.

SANKALPA: A resolve.

SANNYASIN: One who has taken formal vows of renunciation.

SHRADDHA: Care, attentiveness, faith.

SLOKAS: Verses.

SRIMAD BHAGAVATAM: One of the eighteen Mahapuranas or ancient texts of India, containing the life and teachings of Lord Krishna.

TAPAS: Austerity, hardship undergone for the sake of self-purification.

UDDHAVA GITA: A discourse between Lord Krishna and His great devotee, Uddhava. This occurs in the Srimad Bhagavatam by Vyasa.

VASANAS: Residual impressions of objects and actions experienced, habits.

VEDAS: The authoritative scriptures of the Hindus, lit. "Knowledge."

Index